Inner Child Work
Techniques to Heal and Nurture Your Innermost Self

Ellie Bloom

Copyright © 2024 by Ellie Bloom

All rights reserved.

No portion of this book may be reproduced in any form without written permission from the publisher or author, except as permitted by U.S. copyright law.

Contents

1. Introduction to the Concept of the Inner Child — 1
2. Unveiling the Inner Child — 5
3. How Childhood Experiences Shape our Adult Lives — 13
4. Recognizing Inner Child Wounds — 22
5. The Journey to Healing — 32
6. Techniques for Inner Child Healing — 59
7. Overcoming Resistance and Obstacles — 70
8. Building a Nurturing Inner Dialogue — 102
9. The Role of Therapy and Professional Support — 114
10. Integrating the Inner Child in Adult Life — 123
11. Stories of Transformation — 134
12. Conclusion — 139
13. Appendices — 142

Chapter 1

Introduction to the Concept of the Inner Child

In the intriguing matrix of variables of our emotional landscape, the notion of the "inner child" stands as a poignant and profound concept, inviting us to embark on a journey of self-discovery and healing. This metaphorical construct encapsulates the essence of our early experiences, the purity of our emotions, and the untainted curiosity that once defined our perception of the world.

The inner child represents the reservoir of memories, emotions, and beliefs that have been imprinted upon us during our formative years. It embodies the version of ourselves that experienced the world with unfiltered wonder, boundless imagination, and an innate understanding of authenticity. As we navigate the complexities of adulthood, these aspects of our inner child often become buried beneath the layers of responsibilities, societal expectations, and the inevitable trials of life.

Exploring the concept of the inner child invites us to reconnect with these forgotten fragments of our past. It beckons us to peel back the layers of protective armor we've accumulated over the years and rediscover the vulnerable, tender part of ourselves that may have been overshadowed by the demands of adulthood.

Understanding and embracing the inner child is not an exercise in nostalgia but rather a transformative journey toward self-awareness and healing. By acknowledging the wounds and unmet needs of our younger selves, we open the door to profound personal growth and the potential for genuine, lasting change.

Throughout this exploration, we will delve into various aspects of the inner child concept, unraveling the impact of early experiences on our present behaviors, relationships, and emotional well-being. We will navigate the delicate terrain of healing, learning to nurture and re-parent the inner child with compassion and understanding.

As we embark on this introspective journey, let us approach the concept of the inner child with openness, curiosity, and a willingness to embrace the vulnerable parts of ourselves. By doing so, we may unlock the door to a deeper understanding of our authentic selves and cultivate a more compassionate relationship with the past, present, and future.

Join me in this exploration of the inner child—a journey that has the potential to illuminate the path toward greater self-awareness, resilience, and an enriched experience of life.

In the labyrinth of personal growth and emotional healing, the profound impact of inner child work unfolds as a transformative journey. To illuminate the potency of this therapeutic approach, let me share a personal story—a case study that underscores the significance of tending to the inner child.

Meet Sarah, a vibrant woman in her thirties who, on the surface, appeared to have life all figured out. Successful in her career, surrounded by a supportive network of friends, and outwardly confident, Sarah exuded an air of self-assurance. However, beneath the poised exterior lurked a persistent undercurrent of anxiety and a deep-seated fear of abandonment.

As Sarah embarked on her inner child work journey, she discovered that the roots of her emotional struggles were intertwined with the unhealed wounds of her past. Through introspective exercises and guided therapeutic processes, she revisited moments from her childhood that had long been tucked away in the recesses of her memory.

One pivotal memory involved a significant move during her adolescence—a relocation that disrupted her sense of stability and upended familiar connections. Unbeknownst to adult Sarah, the inner child within her clung to the emotions of that turbulent period, fueling her present-day anxieties about abandonment and the impermanence of relationships.

Through the compassionate exploration of her inner child, Sarah began to nurture the wounded aspects of herself that had long yearned for acknowledgment and reassurance. The simple act of recognizing and validating her younger self's emotions opened the door to profound healing. As she embraced her inner child with love and understanding, Sarah found that the grip of anxiety gradually loosened, paving the way for a newfound sense of security and self-assurance.

The impact of Sarah's inner child work extended beyond the realm of her personal relationships. Professionally, she discovered a heightened capacity for resilience and creativity, as the healing of her inner child released dormant wellsprings of authenticity and innovation.

This case study serves as a testament to the potency of inner child work in unraveling the intricacies of our emotional landscapes. By acknowledging and tending to the vulnerable aspects of our past, we create a foundation for lasting healing and personal transformation.

Sarah's journey underscores the importance of embarking on our own exploration of the inner child—a journey that holds the potential to liberate us from the shackles of unresolved pain and illuminate the path toward a more authentic, resilient, and fulfilling life.

Inner Child Work: Techniques to Heal and Nurture Your Innermost Self is not just a book; it's an immersive and compassionate companion on your journey toward self-discovery and emotional healing. Whether you are new to inner child work or seeking to deepen your understanding, this comprehensive guide serves as a roadmap for readers seeking to embark on the empowering path of inner child work, providing insights, practical exercises, and real-life stories to illuminate the way.

Chapter 2
Unveiling the Inner Child

The concept of the "inner child" is a knotty and profound aspect of psychological and emotional well-being. To embark on the journey of healing the inner child, it is essential to first unravel the layers of this metaphorical construct and understand its significance in shaping our present selves.

Defining the Inner Child

The inner child is not a tangible, separate entity within us; rather, it symbolizes the sum of our early experiences, emotions, and beliefs that were imprinted upon us during our formative years. Picture the inner child as the essence of your younger self—the innocent, curious, and emotionally authentic part of you that perceived the world through unfiltered wonder and openness.

Origins of the Inner Child

Rooted in psychoanalytic and psychodynamic theories, the concept of the inner child acknowledges that our early experiences have a lasting impact on our emotional and psychological development. Whether positive or negative, the events of our childhood shape our beliefs about ourselves, others, and the world around us.

Emotional Imprints

Our younger selves, with their unguarded emotions and genuine responses to the world, carry imprints of joy, love, pain, and fear. These imprints influence how we navigate relationships, handle challenges, and perceive our own worth. The inner child holds the emotional residue of past experiences, often manifesting in our adult lives through patterns of behavior and emotional reactions.

The Role of the Inner Child in Adulthood

As we transition into adulthood, the inner child continues to play a pivotal role in our lives. Its presence is felt in our reactions to stress, the way we form and maintain relationships, and our responses to life's challenges. When unhealed, the wounded aspects of the inner child may influence our decisions, self-esteem, and overall well-being.

Nurturing vs. Neglect

Acknowledging the inner child is not about dwelling on past wounds but rather recognizing the need for compassionate attention. Neglecting the inner child can lead to emotional struggles, while nurturing it fosters healing and resilience. By reconnecting with this vulnerable part of ourselves, we open the door to self-discovery, compassion, and transformative growth.

The Inner Child as a Guide

Understanding the inner child is a journey toward self-awareness and emotional liberation. It serves as a guide to unlocking the door to our authentic selves, allowing us to reclaim lost aspects of our identity and rewrite the narrative of our lives.

In the chapters to come, we will delve deeper into the intricacies of the inner child concept, exploring practical approaches to recognizing, nurturing, and healing this integral aspect of ourselves. Through this exploration, we invite the reader to embark on a transformative journey toward a more resilient and authentic existence.

The Psychological Basis of the Inner Child in Human Development

The psychological foundation of the inner child concept lies in the multifaceted interplay of elements of early experiences, cognitive development, and emotional imprinting during the formative years of human development. As we delve into this psychological landscape, it becomes evident how the inner child becomes a profound and enduring aspect of our emotional tapestry.

Cognitive Development

The foundation of the inner child is rooted in the early stages of cognitive development. Piaget's stages of cognitive development highlight the crucial periods during which children construct their understanding of the world. The inner child encapsulates the cognitive and emotional imprints formed during these stages, influencing perceptions and beliefs that persist into adulthood.

Attachment Theory

Attachment theorists, such as John Bowlby, emphasize the importance of early attachment experiences in shaping our interpersonal relationships. The emotional bonds formed with caregivers leave lasting imprints on the inner child, influencing feelings of security, trust, and intimacy in adult relationships.

Psychoanalytic Theories

Freudian and post-Freudian psychoanalytic theories contribute to the understanding of the inner child through concepts like the "id," "ego," and "superego." The inner child, in this context, represents the id—a reservoir of instinctual drives and emotions that form the basis of our personality.

Emotional Imprinting

The inner child concept acknowledges the phenomenon of emotional imprinting, wherein intense emotional experiences during childhood create lasting imprints on our psyche. Positive experiences contribute to a healthy inner child, fostering emotional resilience, while negative experiences may result in wounded aspects that require healing.

Schema Development

Cognitive schemas, developed during childhood, are mental frameworks that shape how we interpret and respond to the world. The inner child carries these schemas into adulthood, influencing perceptions of self, others, and the environment. Unhealthy schemas may contribute to patterns of negative thinking and behavior.

Neuroscience and Plasticity

From a neuroscientific perspective, the brain's plasticity—its ability to adapt and reorganize—supports the concept of the inner child. Neural pathways formed during childhood experiences can be rewired through intentional interventions, allowing for healing and the development of more adaptive responses.

Integration of Emotional Memory

Emotional memories, particularly those associated with significant childhood events, are deeply ingrained in the inner child. These memories shape emotional responses and contribute to the emotional intelligence that influences decision-making and interpersonal dynamics in adulthood.

In essence, the psychological basis of the inner child lies in the profound impact of early experiences on cognitive, emotional, and relational development. By acknowledging and understanding these psychological foundations, we gain insight into the intriguing web of interconnected elements that contribute to the formation and evolution of our inner child—a key component in the journey of self-discovery and healing.

Unraveling Common Misconceptions and Myths About the Inner Child

As we embark on the journey of understanding and healing the inner child, it is crucial to dispel common misconceptions and myths that may cloud our perception. These misconceptions often hinder the transformative potential of inner child work, preventing individuals from fully embracing the healing process.

Myth: The Inner Child is a Literal Entity

Misconception: Some believe that the inner child is a distinct, separate entity within us that needs to be accessed or communicated with in a concrete way.

Reality: The inner child is a metaphorical concept representing our past experiences, emotions, and beliefs. It doesn't have a physical existence but serves as a psychological framework for understanding our emotional landscape.

Myth: Inner Child Work is Only for Those with Traumatic Pasts

Misconception: Inner child work is often perceived as necessary only for individuals with overtly traumatic childhoods.

Reality: Every individual has an inner child, regardless of the nature of their childhood experiences. Inner child work is valuable for anyone seeking self-discovery, healing, and personal growth.

Myth: Healing the Inner Child is a One-Time Process

Misconception: Some believe that addressing the inner child is a one-time endeavor, a quick fix for past wounds.

Reality: Inner child work is an ongoing, iterative process. As we grow and encounter new challenges, revisiting and nurturing the inner child becomes a dynamic part of our lifelong journey.

Myth: It's About Blaming Parents or Caregivers

Misconception: Inner child work is often misunderstood as a process of blaming parents or caregivers for current challenges.

Reality: The focus is on understanding and healing, not assigning blame. It's about recognizing the impact of early experiences and fostering compassion for ourselves and others.

Myth: Inner Child Work is Only for Emotional Healing

Misconception: Inner child work is exclusively associated with emotional healing and has no relevance beyond this realm.

Reality: While emotional healing is a significant aspect, inner child work extends to cognitive, behavioral, and relational dimensions. It influences how we perceive and respond to the world.

Myth: Inner Child Work Requires Regression or Revisiting Traumatic Memories

Misconception: Inner child work is misunderstood as needing to regress to specific traumatic events, causing emotional distress.

Reality: Healing the inner child involves creating a safe space for exploration. It doesn't mandate reliving traumatic events; rather, it encourages understanding and soothing the wounded aspects of the self.

Myth: Inner Child Work is Only for "New Age" or Alternative Approaches

Misconception: Inner child work is sometimes dismissed as a solely "new age" or alternative approach without scientific validity.

Reality: Inner child work aligns with various psychological theories, including attachment theory and psychodynamic approaches. It is widely recognized in therapeutic practices.

By unraveling these common misconceptions, we pave the way for a more accurate and compassionate understanding of the inner child. Recognizing the true nature of inner child work allows individuals to engage in this transformative process with openness, authenticity, and a commitment to holistic well-being.

Chapter 3
How Childhood Experiences Shape our Adult Lives

In the elaborate network of influences of human existence, childhood stands as the foundational loom from which the threads of our adult lives are woven. The experiences we encounter during these formative years leave an indelible mark on our psyche, influencing our beliefs, behaviors, and overall outlook on life. This chapter explores the profound impact that childhood experiences wield over our adult selves, delving into the realms of psychology, neuroscience, and sociology to unravel the complex interaction of factors and connections between past and present.

The Crucible of Childhood

Childhood serves as a crucible where the molten emotions, relationships, and impressions solidify into the core elements of our personalities. The family, often the first crucible we encounter, becomes the initial architect of our identity. Parents, siblings, and caregivers play pivotal roles in shaping our worldview, values, and interpersonal skills. Positive experiences within the family unit can foster a sense of security, trust, and emotional resilience that serves as a robust foundation for adulthood.

Conversely, traumatic or adverse childhood experiences can cast long shadows, affecting various facets of our lives. Childhood trauma, be it physical, emotional, or psychological, can manifest in adulthood through issues like anxiety, depression, or difficulty forming healthy relationships. Understanding the impact of adverse experiences is crucial in breaking the cycle of generational trauma, providing avenues for healing and growth.

The Neurological Imprint

Neuroscience reveals the elaborate network of influences that dance between nature and nurture, as our brains undergo remarkable development during childhood. The brain's plasticity allows it to adapt to the environment, with experiences sculpting neural connections that persist into adulthood. Positive experiences, such as supportive relationships and stimulating environments, contribute to the development of a resilient and well-balanced brain.

Conversely, neglect or trauma can shape the brain in ways that make individuals more susceptible to mental health challenges. The amygdala, responsible for processing emotions, and the prefrontal cortex, crucial for decision-making and impulse control, are particularly vulnerable to the effects of early experiences. Understanding these neural imprints underscores the importance of early intervention and support for children facing adversity.

Socialization and Identity Formation

Beyond the confines of the family, childhood experiences extend into the broader social sphere. Peer interactions, educational environments, and cultural influences contribute to the multifaceted mosaic of our identities. Friendships forged in childhood often leave enduring imprints, influencing our social skills, communication styles, and the ability to trust others.

Cultural and societal norms absorbed during childhood become integral components of our belief systems. These early impressions shape our perspectives on race, gender, and societal roles, influencing our behavior and interactions as adults. Recognizing the impact of cultural and societal influences is essential for fostering inclusivity and dismantling biases that may have taken root during childhood.

Breaking the Chains

While childhood experiences exert a profound influence, they need not dictate the course of our adult lives irrevocably. Awareness, coupled with intentional efforts, can empower individuals to break free from negative patterns and cultivate positive change. Therapy, self-reflection, and supportive relationships provide avenues for healing and growth, allowing individuals to rewrite the narrative of their lives.

In conclusion, the chapters of our childhood lay the foundation upon which the novel of our adult lives is written. Understanding the multidimensional interplay of factors that interplay between experiences, biology, and societal influences enables us to navigate the complexities of adulthood with empathy, resilience, and the potential for transformation. By acknowledging the impact of our early years, we gain insight into the intricacies of our present selves and, in doing so, pave the way for a more intentional and fulfilling future.

The Echoes of Trauma: Bridging Childhood Wounds and Adult Struggles

The echoes of childhood trauma reverberate through the corridors of time, leaving an indelible mark on the psychological landscape of adulthood. The nuanced interplay of variables link between early adversity and adult psychological issues is a field of study that unveils the profound ways in which traumatic experiences can shape the contours of the mind. As we delve into this complex web, it becomes apparent that the wounds inflicted during formative years can cast long shadows, affecting emotional well-being, interpersonal relationships, and overall mental health.

The Neurobiological Impact: A Persistent Symphony of Stress

At the heart of the link between childhood trauma and adult psychological issues lies the intricate interplay within the brain's neurobiological framework. When exposed to trauma, the stress response system activates, flooding the body with hormones designed to cope with immediate threats. In the context of chronic childhood trauma, however, this system can become dysregulated, leading to a heightened and persistent state of arousal.

The hippocampus, responsible for memory consolidation, can be adversely affected, impacting an individual's ability to process and contextualize experiences. Meanwhile, the amygdala, a key player in emotional processing, may become hyperreactive, contributing to heightened emotional responses and difficulty regulating emotions in adulthood. The resulting neurobiological changes lay the groundwork for a range of psychological issues, from anxiety disorders to mood disorders such as depression.

The Blueprint of Attachment: Relationships Marked by Shadows

Childhood trauma often casts a long shadow over the tangled blueprint of attachment—the emotional bond formed between a child and their caregivers. Secure attachment, characterized by trust, safety, and emotional responsiveness, provides a sturdy foundation for healthy relationships in adulthood. Conversely, trauma disrupts this blueprint, leading to insecure or disorganized attachment patterns that may manifest in adult relationships.

Individuals with a history of childhood trauma may struggle with trust issues, intimacy, and forming secure connections. The relational scars of the past can affect the ability to regulate emotions within interpersonal contexts, giving rise to patterns of avoidance or dependence. Recognizing these attachment dynamics is crucial for individuals seeking to navigate the complexities of adult relationships and build connections based on security and mutual support.

Cycles of Self-Perception: From Powerlessness to Empowerment

The aftermath of childhood trauma often leaves a lasting imprint on self-perception, shaping the narrative individuals construct about their own worth and agency. The powerlessness experienced during traumatic events can morph into a persistent sense of vulnerability, inadequacy, or shame in adulthood. The internalized messages of helplessness may contribute to the development of maladaptive coping mechanisms, such as substance abuse, self-harm, or patterns of self-sabotage.

Breaking free from these cycles requires a profound journey of self-discovery and healing. Therapy, whether cognitive-behavioral, psychodynamic, or trauma-focused, can serve as a compass guiding individuals through the labyrinth of their own psyche. By unraveling the threads of past trauma and reconstructing a narrative of resilience and empowerment, individuals can redefine their self-perception and forge a path toward psychological well-being.

Illuminate, Understand, Heal: The Path Forward

Understanding the link between childhood trauma and adult psychological issues is not a mere exercise in introspection but a crucial step toward healing. Shedding light on the shadows cast by early adversity allows individuals to confront and process their experiences. Therapy, support networks, and mindfulness practices offer avenues for navigating the emotional terrain shaped by childhood trauma, fostering resilience and reclaiming agency over one's narrative.

In the journey from the echoes of trauma to the restoration of mental well-being, individuals can rewrite the script of their lives. The link between childhood wounds and adult struggles need not be a binding chain but rather a roadmap toward understanding, growth, and ultimately, healing.

Case studies and examples

Case Study 1: Sarah's Struggle with Anxiety and Perfectionism

Sarah, a successful professional in her early thirties, sought therapy for severe anxiety and perfectionism that were hindering her personal and work life. Through therapy, it was revealed that Sarah experienced emotional neglect during her childhood. Her parents, though physically present, were emotionally unavailable, leaving Sarah to navigate her emotions in isolation. As an adult, Sarah's fear of failure and relentless pursuit of perfection were rooted in her childhood experiences. Therapy focused on addressing these deep-seated issues, helping Sarah develop healthier coping mechanisms and fostering self-compassion.

Case Study 2: Mark's Journey from Childhood Abuse to Adult Substance Abuse

Mark, a middle-aged man struggling with substance abuse, traced the origins of his addiction back to a traumatic childhood marked by physical abuse. The trauma left Mark with feelings of powerlessness and low self-worth. As an adult, he turned to substances to cope with the pain and numb the emotional scars of his past. In rehabilitation, Mark underwent trauma-focused therapy, addressing the root causes of his addiction. By understanding the connection between his childhood trauma and substance abuse, he began the process of healing and building a foundation for a healthier future.

Case Study 3: Emily's Patterns of Dysfunctional Relationships

Emily, in her late twenties, faced persistent challenges in forming and maintaining healthy relationships. Through therapy, it became evident that Emily's parents had a tumultuous marriage, marked by emotional volatility and neglect. As a child, Emily internalized these patterns, and as an adult, she struggled to establish secure attachments. Therapy focused on breaking the cycle of dysfunctional relationship patterns, helping Emily recognize and challenge her ingrained beliefs about love and connection. Over time, she learned to form healthier relationships built on trust and communication.

Case Study 4: David's Journey from Childhood Trauma to PTSD

David, a military veteran, sought therapy for symptoms of post-traumatic stress disorder (PTSD). As a child, David experienced significant trauma through domestic violence in his family. These early experiences of fear and unpredictability set the stage for his vulnerability to trauma later in life. The therapy involved a combination of trauma-focused approaches and cognitive-behavioral techniques to help David process the traumatic memories and develop coping strategies. Understanding the link between his childhood trauma and adult PTSD was pivotal in David's journey toward healing.

Case Study 5: Rachel's Struggle with Depression and Self-Esteem

Rachel, a woman in her forties, grappled with chronic depression and low self-esteem. In therapy, it was revealed that Rachel grew up in a household where emotional expression was discouraged, and her achievements were rarely acknowledged. As an adult, she internalized feelings of inadequacy and struggled to find joy in her accomplishments. Therapy focused on re-framing Rachel's self-perception, addressing the impact of her childhood experiences on her self-esteem, and fostering a more positive and realistic view of herself.

These case studies illustrate the diverse ways in which childhood trauma can manifest in adult psychological issues. Each person's journey is unique, and understanding the link between past experiences and present struggles is a crucial step in the process of healing and transformation.

Chapter 4

Recognizing Inner Child Wounds

In the mazelike dance of human psychology, the inner child represents the essence of our earliest experiences, emotions, and wounds. When these wounds go unhealed, the inner child continues to cast its influence on our adult lives, subtly shaping our thoughts, behaviors, and relationships. This chapter explores the signs that may indicate the presence of an unhealed inner child, providing a roadmap for self-discovery and the journey toward healing.

Patterns of Self-Sabotage and Perfectionism

An unhealed inner child often manifests in patterns of self-sabotage and perfectionism. The inner child, seeking validation and approval, may drive individuals to set unrealistic standards for themselves. Perfectionism becomes a shield against the fear of rejection or criticism, but it also perpetuates a cycle of frustration and self-blame when these unattainable goals are not met.

Difficulty in Establishing and Maintaining Relationships

The inner child's wounds can echo through adult relationships. Fear of abandonment, trust issues, or an excessive need for validation may manifest in difficulties forming and sustaining healthy connections. Recognizing patterns of emotional unavailability, excessive clinginess, or a tendency to recreate past relational dynamics can be indicative of an unhealed inner child.

Chronic Self-Doubt and Low Self-Esteem

A wounded inner child often whispers messages of inadequacy and self-doubt. Individuals with an unhealed inner child may struggle with chronic feelings of unworthiness, despite external achievements. Identifying persistent negative self-talk, feelings of shame, and an inability to celebrate personal accomplishments can be crucial in understanding and addressing these inner wounds.

Repetitive Negative Relationship Patterns

Unresolved childhood issues can create a blueprint for adult relationships. Individuals may find themselves repeatedly attracted to partners who mirror the dynamics of their early caregivers, whether it be through emotional unavailability, manipulation, or neglect. Recognizing and breaking these patterns is essential for breaking free from the grip of the unhealed inner child.

Fear of Abandonment and Rejection

The fear of abandonment, rooted in unmet childhood needs, can cast a long shadow over adult life. Individuals with an unhealed inner child may exhibit intense anxiety or avoidance in response to perceived threats of abandonment. This fear can impact decision-making, communication, and the ability to form secure attachments.

Difficulty Expressing Emotions and Setting Boundaries

An unhealed inner child often struggles with emotional expression and setting boundaries. Suppressing emotions or lacking the ability to assert one's needs can be indicative of unresolved childhood wounds. Recognizing the difficulty in navigating and communicating emotions, as well as setting healthy boundaries, is a crucial step toward healing.

Escapism and Addictive Behaviors

The unhealed inner child may seek refuge in escapism and addictive behaviors as a coping mechanism. Whether through substance abuse, excessive work, or other compulsive behaviors, these patterns often serve as a temporary escape from the emotional pain carried from childhood. Acknowledging these coping mechanisms is vital for addressing the root cause.

Persistent Feelings of Emptiness or Loneliness

A wounded inner child may contribute to an enduring sense of emptiness or loneliness. Despite external achievements or relationships, individuals may grapple with an underlying sense of incompleteness. Exploring and understanding these feelings can unveil the unresolved needs of the inner child.

Conclusion: Nurturing the Inner Child to Heal and Thrive

Identifying the signs of an unhealed inner child is the first step on the path to healing. Recognizing these patterns allows individuals to embark on a journey of self-discovery, self-compassion, and intentional healing. Therapy, self-reflection, and compassionate self-care are powerful tools in nurturing the inner child, fostering a sense of wholeness, and reclaiming agency over one's narrative. As we shine a light on the lingering echoes of the past, we pave the way for a future marked by resilience, authenticity, and the transformative power of self-love.

Unraveling the Tapestry - Common Emotional and Behavioral Patterns Stemming from Inner Child Wounds

The inner child, that vulnerable and tender part of our psyche shaped by early experiences, weaves a complex tapestry that influences our emotional and behavioral responses as adults. Understanding the common patterns that stem from inner child wounds is a key to unraveling the intricacies of our present selves. In this chapter, we explore these patterns, shedding light on the emotional landscapes and behavioral scripts etched by the imprints of our early years.

1. Fear of Abandonment and Clinging to Relationships

Emotional Pattern: The fear of abandonment, rooted in unmet childhood needs, often manifests as an intense clinging to relationships. Individuals may struggle with deep-seated anxieties about being left alone or unloved, leading to a persistent need for reassurance and closeness.

Behavioral Pattern: In relationships, this may translate into a constant need for validation, excessive dependency, or an overwhelming fear of rejection. The individual may go to great lengths to avoid perceived abandonment, even at the expense of personal boundaries.

2. Difficulty Trusting Others and Building Intimacy

Emotional Pattern: A history of betrayal or unfulfilled emotional needs during childhood can cultivate a pervasive difficulty in trusting others. The inner child, scarred by past wounds, may remain guarded and hesitant to open up emotionally.

Behavioral Pattern: This emotional pattern often results in challenges forming deep, meaningful connections. Individuals may struggle to express vulnerability or share their authentic selves, maintaining a protective barrier to prevent potential emotional harm.

3. Perfectionism and Relentless Self-Criticism

Emotional Pattern: An unhealed inner child may internalize unrealistic expectations and standards, leading to a persistent fear of failure and a need for external validation.

Behavioral Pattern: Perfectionism becomes a shield against the perceived threat of criticism or rejection. Individuals may engage in relentless self-criticism, never feeling good enough despite external accomplishments. This pattern can lead to chronic stress and burnout.

4. Difficulty Expressing and Managing Emotions

Emotional Pattern: Suppressed or unacknowledged emotions from childhood can contribute to difficulties expressing and managing emotions in adulthood.

Behavioral Pattern: Individuals may find it challenging to articulate their feelings or navigate emotional landscapes. This can lead to emotional outbursts, emotional numbness, or the use of maladaptive coping mechanisms to avoid confronting difficult emotions.

5. People-Pleasing and Difficulty Setting Boundaries

Emotional Pattern: A desire for approval and acceptance, often stemming from unmet childhood needs, can result in a people-pleasing tendency.

Behavioral Pattern: Individuals may habitually prioritize others' needs over their own, neglecting personal boundaries. This pattern can lead to feelings of resentment, exhaustion, and a diminished sense of self.

6. Escapism and Addictive Behaviors

Emotional Pattern: The inner child, seeking relief from emotional pain, may foster a proclivity towards escapism.

Behavioral Pattern: This can manifest in various addictive behaviors such as substance abuse, compulsive shopping, or excessive engagement in activities as a means to numb or avoid confronting underlying emotional wounds.

7. Chronic Self-Doubt and Imposter Syndrome

Emotional Pattern: A history of invalidated feelings or experiences can contribute to chronic self-doubt and a persistent fear of being exposed as a fraud.

Behavioral Pattern: Individuals may struggle with imposter syndrome, doubting their abilities and fearing that they will be unmasked as inadequate. Despite external evidence of competence, the inner child's doubts persist.

8. Reliving Childhood Dynamics in Adult Relationships

Emotional Pattern: Unresolved childhood dynamics often find their way into adult relationships, creating a blueprint for interaction.

Behavioral Pattern: Individuals may unknowingly recreate familiar relational patterns, choosing partners or engaging in behaviors reminiscent of their caregivers. Breaking free from these patterns requires conscious awareness and intentional efforts in therapy or self-reflection.

Conclusion: A Path to Healing and Transformation

Recognizing these common emotional and behavioral patterns born from inner child wounds is the first step towards a transformative journey of healing. By unraveling the tapestry woven by the inner child, individuals can embark on a path of self-discovery, self-compassion, and intentional growth. Therapy, mindfulness practices, and self-reflection serve as powerful tools for rewriting the scripts that no longer serve, fostering resilience, and cultivating a future marked by authenticity, emotional freedom, and a profound connection with one's true self.

Recognizing Inner Child Wounds: Self-Assessment Questionnaire

Instructions: Consider each statement and rate how strongly you identify with it on a scale from 1 to 5, where 1 is "Strongly Disagree" and 5 is "Strongly Agree."

1. Fear of Abandonment:

- I often worry that people will leave me.

- I feel intense anxiety when I'm not in constant contact with loved ones.

- I find it difficult to trust that others will stay in my life.

2. Trust and Intimacy:

- I struggle to open up emotionally in relationships.

- I find it challenging to trust others, especially with my deepest feelings.

- I fear being vulnerable and being hurt emotionally.

3. Perfectionism and Self-Criticism:

    - I set very high standards for myself and feel upset if I don't meet them.
    - I often criticize myself for not being good enough.
    - I feel a constant pressure to achieve more.

4. Difficulty Expressing Emotions:

    - I find it hard to identify and express my emotions.
    - I often feel overwhelmed by my emotions.
    - I tend to suppress my feelings to avoid conflict.

5. People-Pleasing and Boundary Issues:

    - I often prioritize others' needs over my own.
    - I struggle to say "no" and establish clear boundaries.
    - I fear that setting boundaries will lead to rejection.

6. Escapism and Addictive Behaviors:

    - I engage in activities to numb or avoid difficult emotions.
    - I sometimes use substances (e.g., alcohol, drugs) to cope with emotional pain.
    - I feel a constant need to distract myself from my thoughts and feelings.

7. Chronic Self-Doubt and Imposter Syndrome:

- I frequently doubt my abilities, despite evidence of competence.
- I fear that others will discover I'm not as capable as they think.
- I often attribute my success to luck rather than my skills.

8. Reliving Childhood Dynamics in Relationships:

- I notice similarities between my current relationships and those from my childhood.
- I find myself repeating patterns from my family of origin in my relationships.
- I struggle to create healthier dynamics in my current relationships.

Scoring: Add up your scores for each section. The higher the total score, the more likely it is that you may have unresolved inner child wounds. Remember that this self-assessment is not a diagnostic tool, but rather a guide for self-reflection. If you find yourself identifying with many of these statements, seeking the support of a mental health professional or engaging in further self-exploration could be beneficial.

Chapter 5

The Journey to Healing

Nurturing Wholeness - An Overview of the Healing Process

Embarking on the journey of healing, particularly when addressing inner child wounds, is a profound and transformative endeavor. This chapter provides an overview of the healing process, guiding individuals through the essential stages of self-discovery, acceptance, and intentional growth. Understanding the intricacies of healing empowers individuals to embark on a path toward reclaiming their authentic selves and fostering emotional well-being.

Acknowledging the Wounds

Acknowledging the wounds of inner child work is an essential step on the path to healing and self-discovery. Our inner child represents the vulnerable and impressionable aspects of ourselves that were shaped by childhood experiences, both positive and negative. These wounds often manifest as deep-seated emotional pain, insecurities, and patterns of behavior that continue to influence our adult lives.

By acknowledging these wounds, we begin to shine a light on the hidden corners of our psyche, allowing us to confront and address the unresolved issues from our past.

At the heart of inner child work lies the recognition that the wounds we carry were not of our own making. They are the result of circumstances beyond our control, shaped by the environment in which we were raised and the experiences we encountered along the way. By acknowledging these wounds with compassion and empathy, we can begin to untangle the complex web of emotions that have held us captive for so long.

Acknowledging the wounds of our inner child is a courageous act of self-love and self-compassion. It requires us to confront painful memories and emotions that we may have buried deep within ourselves. Yet, it is only by acknowledging and embracing these wounds that we can begin the process of healing and transformation. By extending kindness and understanding to our inner child, we create a safe and nurturing space in which healing can take place.

In acknowledging the wounds of our inner child, we also reclaim our power and agency. Rather than allowing past traumas to dictate our present reality, we take ownership of our experiences and begin to rewrite the narrative of our lives. This process of acknowledgment is not about dwelling on the past or assigning blame, but rather about recognizing the impact that our experiences have had on us and taking steps to cultivate healing and resilience. In doing so, we open ourselves up to the possibility of profound personal growth and transformation, reclaiming our authentic selves and embracing the fullness of who we are.

Self-Reflection and Exploration

Self-reflection and exploration are fundamental aspects of inner child work, providing a pathway to understanding and healing the wounds of our past. Through self-reflection, we embark on a journey of introspection, delving into the depths of our psyche to uncover the hidden layers of our inner child. This process allows us to identify patterns of behavior, thought, and emotion that have been shaped by childhood experiences, offering insight into the origins of our present-day struggles.

Journaling is a powerful tool for self-reflection in inner child work, providing a safe and private space to explore our thoughts, feelings, and memories. By putting pen to paper, we can give voice to the voiceless parts of ourselves, allowing our inner child to express its fears, desires, and pain. Through journaling, we can gain clarity and perspective on our experiences, tracking patterns and themes that emerge over time. This practice fosters a deeper connection with our inner selves, enabling us to cultivate greater self-awareness and insight.

Therapeutic support plays a crucial role in facilitating self-reflection and exploration in inner child work. A skilled therapist provides guidance, validation, and support as we navigate the often challenging terrain of our inner world. Through compassionate listening and empathetic understanding, therapists create a safe and nurturing space in which we can explore our inner child with courage and vulnerability. They offer tools and techniques to aid in self-reflection, guiding us through exercises and prompts designed to uncover deeper layers of our psyche.

In the presence of therapeutic support, we are encouraged to confront difficult emotions and memories that may arise during the process of inner child work. Through gentle guidance and encouragement, therapists help us navigate these emotions with compassion and resilience, fostering a sense of empowerment and self-acceptance. Together, therapist and client work collaboratively to explore the wounds of the inner child, gently unraveling the layers of pain and uncovering the seeds of healing beneath. Through this journey of self-reflection and exploration, we pave the way for profound personal growth and transformation, reclaiming our authentic selves and embracing the fullness of who we are.

Reconnecting with the Inner Child

Reconnecting with the inner child is a transformative journey that allows us to heal past wounds and nurture the vulnerable aspects of ourselves. Visualization serves as a powerful tool in this process, enabling us to access the deeper realms of our psyche and connect with our inner child on an emotional level. Through guided imagery, we can visualize ourselves as children, revisiting significant moments from our past and offering comfort and reassurance to our younger selves. By creating a safe and loving space in our minds, we can foster a sense of compassion and understanding towards the inner child, laying the groundwork for healing and growth.

Inner dialogue is another essential component of reconnecting with the inner child. Through introspective reflection and self-talk, we can engage in a compassionate dialogue with our inner child, acknowledging its fears, needs, and desires. By listening attentively to the inner voice of the child within, we can validate its experiences and offer words of comfort and encouragement. This inner dialogue helps to bridge the gap between our adult selves and our inner child, fostering a deeper sense of connection and integration.

Mindfulness practices play a vital role in reconnecting with the inner child by cultivating present-moment awareness and attunement to our inner experiences. Through mindfulness meditation, we can observe the thoughts, emotions, and sensations that arise within us without judgment or resistance. This practice allows us to become more attuned to the needs and desires of our inner child, creating space for healing and transformation. By cultivating mindfulness, we can develop a greater sense of inner peace and harmony, nurturing the wounded aspects of ourselves with compassion and acceptance.

Expressive arts offer a creative outlet for reconnecting with the inner child, allowing us to express our emotions and experiences through various artistic mediums. Whether through painting, drawing, writing, or movement, expressive arts provide a means of accessing the deeper layers of our psyche and giving voice to the inner child. By engaging in creative expression, we can tap into the subconscious mind and unearth buried emotions and memories, fostering catharsis and healing. Through the act of creation, we can reconnect with the innocence, wonder, and creativity of our inner child, fostering a sense of joy and playfulness in our lives.

Incorporating visualization, inner dialogue, mindfulness practices, and expressive arts into our daily routine can help us reconnect with the inner child and embark on a journey of healing and self-discovery. By creating a safe and nurturing space for our inner child to express itself, we can cultivate greater self-awareness, resilience, and compassion. Through this process of reconnecting with the inner child, we can reclaim our sense of wholeness and authenticity, embracing the fullness of who we are with love and acceptance.

Setting Boundaries and Self-Care

Setting boundaries and prioritizing self-care are crucial aspects of inner child work, providing a foundation for healing and growth. When engaging in inner child work, it's essential to establish clear boundaries to protect ourselves from re-traumatization and overwhelm. Setting boundaries involves identifying our needs, limits, and values, and communicating them assertively with others and ourselves. By establishing healthy boundaries, we create a safe and supportive environment for our inner child to explore and express itself without fear of judgment or harm.

Self-care is an integral part of inner child work, as it involves nurturing and tending to our own emotional, physical, and spiritual well-being. Practicing self-care allows us to replenish our energy reserves, reduce stress, and cultivate a sense of balance and harmony in our lives. This may involve engaging in activities that bring us joy and fulfillment, such as spending time in nature, practicing mindfulness, or engaging in creative expression. By prioritizing self-care, we honor the needs of our inner child and create space for healing and growth to unfold.

In the context of inner child work, setting boundaries and practicing self-care go hand in hand. Setting boundaries helps us create a protective container for our inner child to explore and process emotions safely, while self-care provides the nourishment and support needed to sustain us on our healing journey. Together, these practices create a solid foundation for inner child work, enabling us to navigate the complexities of our inner world with greater ease and resilience.

However, setting boundaries and practicing self-care in inner child work can sometimes be challenging, especially for those who have experienced trauma or neglect in childhood. Past experiences may have left us with a sense of unworthiness or guilt when it comes to prioritizing our own needs. In these instances, it's important to approach boundary-setting and self-care with compassion and patience, acknowledging that healing is a process that takes time and effort.

Ultimately, setting boundaries and practicing self-care in inner child work is an act of self-love and empowerment. By honoring our needs and prioritizing our well-being, we create a nurturing environment in which our inner child can thrive and flourish. As we cultivate a deeper sense of self-awareness and self-compassion, we pave the way for healing and transformation to unfold, allowing us to reclaim our sense of wholeness and authenticity with love and acceptance.

Rewriting Limiting Beliefs

Rewriting limiting beliefs is a transformative process that involves identifying and challenging the negative thought patterns that hold us back from reaching our full potential. These beliefs often stem from past experiences, societal conditioning, or negative self-talk, and can manifest as thoughts such as "I'm not good enough," "I'll never succeed," or "I don't deserve happiness." By identifying these limiting beliefs, we can begin to unravel the stories we tell ourselves about our capabilities and worth.

Cognitive restructuring, a key component of rewriting limiting beliefs, involves replacing negative thought patterns with more positive and empowering ones. This process requires us to examine the evidence supporting our beliefs and challenge their validity. Through cognitive restructuring, we can reframe our thoughts, shifting from self-criticism to self-compassion, and from doubt to confidence. By consciously choosing to focus on more empowering beliefs, we can create a new narrative that aligns with our goals and aspirations.

The benefits of cognitive restructuring are far-reaching and profound. By rewriting limiting beliefs, we free ourselves from the constraints of self-doubt and negativity, allowing us to cultivate a greater sense of self-worth and resilience. As we challenge and replace negative thought patterns with more empowering ones, we begin to change the way we perceive ourselves and the world around us. This shift in mindset opens up new possibilities and opportunities for personal growth and success.

Moreover, cognitive restructuring can have a positive impact on our emotional well-being, helping to reduce stress, anxiety, and depression. By reframing our thoughts and focusing on more positive and constructive beliefs, we can cultivate a greater sense of optimism and hope. This, in turn, allows us to approach challenges with greater confidence and resilience, knowing that we have the inner resources to overcome obstacles and achieve our goals.

In essence, rewriting limiting beliefs through cognitive restructuring is a powerful tool for personal transformation and growth. By identifying and challenging negative thought patterns, we can create a new narrative that empowers us to live authentically and pursue our dreams with confidence and purpose. As we embrace more empowering beliefs about ourselves and our abilities, we open ourselves up to a world of possibilities, allowing us to live more fully and vibrantly.

Inner Child Reparenting

Inner child reparenting is a deeply healing process that involves nurturing and caring for the wounded aspects of our inner child that may not have received adequate love, support, or validation during our formative years. This approach recognizes that many of the challenges we face in adulthood stem from unmet needs and unresolved emotions from childhood. By reparenting our inner child, we seek to provide the love, understanding, and guidance that was missing during our upbringing.

Meeting unmet needs is a central aspect of inner child reparenting. This involves identifying the emotional and psychological needs that were not adequately addressed in childhood and taking steps to fulfill them in the present. For example, if we experienced a lack of emotional support growing up, we can offer ourselves compassion and validation as adults. By acknowledging and validating our own feelings, we can begin to heal the wounds of neglect and abandonment that may still linger from childhood.

Parenting yourself is another key component of inner child reparenting. This involves adopting the role of a nurturing and supportive parent to your inner child, offering guidance, encouragement, and protection. Just as a loving parent would care for their child's physical, emotional, and spiritual well-being, we can provide ourselves with the same level of care and attention. This may involve setting healthy boundaries, practicing self-compassion, and engaging in self-care activities that nourish our body, mind, and soul.

Through inner child reparenting, we can cultivate a deeper sense of self-love, acceptance, and resilience. By acknowledging and addressing the unmet needs of our inner child, we can heal the wounds of our past and create a more nurturing and supportive inner environment.

As we learn to parent ourselves with kindness and compassion, we can break free from the cycle of self-criticism and self-sabotage, paving the way for greater emotional well-being and personal growth. Ultimately, inner child reparenting empowers us to reclaim our inner child and embrace the fullness of who we are with love and acceptance.

Integration and Transformation

Integration and transformation are the natural outcomes of inner child work, as we embark on a journey of healing and self-discovery. Through this process, we seek to integrate the wounded aspects of our inner child with our adult selves, fostering a sense of wholeness and authenticity. Integration involves acknowledging and accepting all parts of ourselves, including the painful memories and emotions that may arise during inner child work. By embracing these aspects of our inner child with compassion and understanding, we create space for healing and growth to unfold.

As we engage in inner child work, we undergo a profound transformation, both internally and externally. We begin to release old patterns of thought and behavior that no longer serve us, making way for new insights and perspectives to emerge. This transformation involves a deepening of self-awareness and self-compassion, as we learn to navigate the complexities of our inner world with greater ease and resilience. By embracing change, we open ourselves up to the possibilities of personal growth and evolution, allowing ourselves to become the best versions of ourselves.

Celebrating progress is an essential part of the inner child work journey, as we acknowledge the courage and resilience it takes to confront our past and embrace our inner child with love and acceptance. Each step forward, no matter how small, is a cause for celebration, as it represents a milestone on the path to healing and transformation. By recognizing and honoring our progress, we reinforce our commitment to inner child work and empower ourselves to continue on the path of self-discovery and growth.

Integration and transformation are ongoing processes that unfold over time, requiring patience, dedication, and self-compassion. As we continue to engage in inner child work, we deepen our connection with ourselves and with others, fostering a greater sense of empathy, authenticity, and wholeness. By embracing change and celebrating our progress along the way, we can fully embody the transformative power of inner child work, reclaiming our inner child and embracing the fullness of who we are with love and acceptance.

Conclusion: A Continual Journey of Self-Discovery

Healing from inner child wounds is not a linear process but a continual journey of self-discovery and growth. Each stage of healing contributes to a greater understanding of oneself and paves the way for a more fulfilling and authentic life. The healing process is an act of self-love and resilience, allowing individuals to reclaim their wholeness and move forward with newfound strength and compassion.

The Crucial Prelude - Acknowledging and Accepting the Inner Child

In the sophisticated interplay of components of self-discovery and healing, the acknowledgment and acceptance of the inner child stand as foundational pillars. Before embarking on the journey of transformation, it is paramount to recognize and embrace the vulnerable, tender part of ourselves that carries the imprints of early experiences. This portion of the chapter delves into the profound importance of acknowledging and accepting the inner child as the critical prelude to a path of healing and personal growth.

Understanding the Roots of the Self:

Understanding the roots of the self is a foundational aspect of inner child work, as it involves delving into the early experiences and relationships that shaped our sense of identity and self-worth. By exploring the roots of our self-concept, we gain insight into the origins of our beliefs, behaviors, and emotional patterns. This process allows us to uncover the deep-seated wounds and unmet needs of our inner child, which may have been formed during childhood experiences such as neglect, abandonment, or trauma.

As we delve into the roots of the self through inner child work, we begin to unravel the complex interplay between our past and present selves. We come to understand how our early experiences continue to influence our thoughts, feelings, and actions in adulthood, often without our conscious awareness. By shining a light on these hidden dynamics, we can begin to untangle the knots of our inner world and create space for healing and growth to occur.

Through inner child work, we cultivate a deeper understanding and acceptance of ourselves, embracing all aspects of our being with compassion and empathy. By acknowledging the roots of our self-concept, we gain a greater sense of agency and empowerment, as we recognize that we have the power to rewrite our own narrative and create a more fulfilling and authentic life. As we continue on the journey of inner child work, we honor the roots of our self with love and acceptance, paving the way for profound personal transformation and self-discovery.

Validation and Compassion:

Validation and compassion are essential elements of inner child healing work, providing a nurturing and supportive foundation for the process of self-discovery and growth. Validation involves acknowledging and accepting the feelings and experiences of our inner child without judgment or criticism. By validating our emotions, we create a safe and supportive environment

in which our inner child feels heard, understood, and accepted.

Compassion is the heart of inner child healing work, as it involves extending kindness, understanding, and empathy towards ourselves and our inner child. Through compassion, we offer ourselves the same level of care and compassion that we would offer to a dear friend or loved one. This practice allows us to hold space for our inner child with gentleness and tenderness, fostering a sense of safety and trust that is essential for healing to occur.

In the context of inner child healing work, validation and compassion go hand in hand. By validating our emotions and experiences with compassion, we create a nurturing inner environment in which our inner child feels supported and cared for. This sense of validation and compassion allows us to heal the wounds of our past, releasing the pain and suffering that have held us back from living fully and authentically.

Through the practice of validation and compassion in inner child healing work, we cultivate a deeper sense of self-love and acceptance. By offering ourselves validation and compassion, we learn to embrace all aspects of ourselves with kindness and understanding, fostering a greater sense of wholeness and inner peace. As we continue on the journey of inner child healing work, validation and compassion serve as guiding principles, leading us towards greater self-discovery, healing, and transformation.

Breaking the Cycle of Self-Abandonment:

Breaking the cycle of self-abandonment is a crucial aspect of inner child healing work, as it involves recognizing and addressing the ways in which we neglect or disregard our own needs and emotions. Self-abandonment often stems from early childhood experiences of neglect, rejection, or invalidation, which can leave us feeling unworthy or undeserving of love and care. Through inner child healing work, we can begin to unravel these patterns of self-abandonment and cultivate a deeper sense of self-love and acceptance.

One of the first steps in breaking the cycle of self-abandonment is to recognize and acknowledge the ways in which we abandon ourselves. This may involve reflecting on past experiences and identifying the thought patterns and behaviors that contribute to feelings of self-neglect or self-criticism. By bringing awareness to these patterns, we can begin to take steps towards self-compassion and self-care, nurturing the wounded aspects of our inner child with kindness and understanding.

In inner child healing work, breaking the cycle of self-abandonment also involves re-parenting ourselves with love and compassion. This means learning to listen to our own needs and emotions, and responding to them with care and empathy. By practicing self-compassion and self-care, we can begin to heal the wounds of self-abandonment and cultivate a deeper sense of self-worth and resilience. As we break free from the cycle of self-abandonment, we open ourselves up to a new way of relating to ourselves and the world, one that is rooted in love, acceptance, and self-empowerment.

Empowering Self-Discovery:

Empowering self-discovery lies at the heart of inner child healing work, as it involves uncovering the hidden aspects of ourselves and reclaiming our innate worth and power. Through inner child healing work, we embark on a journey of self-exploration and self-awareness, delving into the depths of our psyche to uncover the root causes of our pain and suffering. This process allows us to shed light on the limiting beliefs and patterns of behavior that have held us back from living fully and authentically.

As we engage in inner child healing work, we empower ourselves to break free from the chains of the past and step into a new paradigm of self-discovery and growth. Through practices such as self-reflection, mindfulness, and creative expression, we cultivate a deeper understanding of ourselves and our inner world. This newfound self-awareness allows us to make conscious choices that align with our values and aspirations, empowering us to create the life we desire with courage and intention.

Fostering Emotional Integration:

Fostering emotional integration is a central goal of inner child work, as it involves acknowledging, accepting, and integrating the full spectrum of our emotions. Often, our inner child holds onto unresolved feelings from the past, such as pain, anger, sadness, or fear. Through inner child work, we create a safe space to explore and express these emotions, allowing them to be seen, heard, and validated. By embracing our emotions with compassion and understanding, we pave the way for emotional integration and healing to occur.

One of the key ways to foster emotional integration in inner child work is through mindfulness practices. Mindfulness invites us to observe our emotions without judgment or attachment, allowing them to arise and pass away like clouds in the sky. By cultivating present-moment awareness, we can develop a greater capacity to sit with uncomfortable emotions and navigate them with grace and resilience. Through mindfulness, we learn to befriend our emotions and cultivate a sense of equanimity in the face of life's challenges.

Another important aspect of fostering emotional integration in inner child work is through expressive arts therapies. Creative modalities such as art, writing, music, and movement offer powerful channels for exploring and expressing our emotions in a non-verbal way. Through creative expression, we can access the deeper layers of our psyche and give voice to the unspoken truths of our inner world. This process allows us to release pent-up emotions, gain insight into our experiences, and cultivate greater self-awareness and healing.

In addition to mindfulness and expressive arts therapies, fostering emotional integration in inner child work also involves cultivating self-compassion and self-acceptance. By offering ourselves kindness and understanding, we create a nurturing inner environment in which all emotions are welcome and accepted. This sense of self-compassion allows us to embrace the fullness of our emotional experience with love and acceptance, paving the way for greater emotional integration and well-being. Ultimately, fostering emotional integration in inner child work allows us to reclaim our wholeness and authenticity, embracing the richness of our emotional landscape with courage and grace.

Building Bridges to Healing:

Building bridges to healing in inner child work involves creating pathways for communication, understanding, and reconciliation between our present-day selves and our inner child. This process begins with acknowledging and validating the experiences of our inner child, recognizing the impact that past traumas and wounds have had on our present-day lives. By extending compassion and empathy towards our inner child, we create a foundation of trust and safety that is essential for healing to occur.

Once the bridge of understanding has been established, inner child work invites us to engage in practices that promote healing and integration. This may involve various therapeutic modalities such as journaling, visualization, expressive arts, and somatic experiencing, each offering unique opportunities for exploration and self-expression. Through these practices, we can begin to release the emotional baggage of the past, cultivate self-awareness, and foster greater resilience and well-being.

Building bridges to healing in inner child work also requires patience, perseverance, and self-compassion. Healing is not a linear process, and there may be times when progress feels slow or stagnant. By practicing self-compassion and gentleness with ourselves, we create space for healing to unfold at its own pace. As we continue to nurture the connection with our inner child and engage in practices that promote healing and integration, we build bridges that lead us towards greater wholeness, authenticity, and inner peace.

Conclusion: The Transformative Power of Recognition:

In the dance of self-discovery, acknowledgment and acceptance of the inner child are not mere formalities but potent catalysts for transformation. It is a call to embrace the self with open arms, acknowledging the scars and vulnerabilities as integral parts of the tapestry that makes each individual uniquely human. As we embark on this journey, let us carry with us the wisdom that in acknowledging the inner child, we unlock the door to profound healing, self-love, and the reclamation of our authentic selves.

Tender Mercies: Emotional Support and Self-Compassion in the Healing Process

In the labyrinth of healing, emotional support and self-compassion serve as guiding lights, illuminating the path towards transformation. This chapter explores the profound impact of cultivating emotional support systems and practicing self-compassion as essential components of the healing journey. As we navigate the complexities of healing, we discover that extending kindness to ourselves and fostering supportive connections can be potent remedies for wounds that resonate from the depths of the inner child.

Building a Foundation of Emotional Support

Building a foundation of emotional support in inner child work begins with identifying our supportive needs and understanding what makes us feel safe, validated, and nurtured. This process involves deep introspection and self-awareness, as we explore the emotions and experiences that trigger feelings of vulnerability or discomfort. By identifying our supportive needs, such as the need for validation, empathy, or reassurance, we can begin to communicate these needs to ourselves and others, creating a supportive environment for our inner child to thrive.

Effective communication of our supportive needs is essential in building a foundation of emotional support in inner child work. This involves expressing our emotions, desires, and boundaries assertively and authentically. By communicating our needs with clarity and honesty, we create opportunities for connection and understanding with ourselves and others. Through open and honest communication, we can foster deeper relationships, build trust, and create a sense of safety and security that is essential for inner child healing.

Furthermore, building a foundation of emotional support in inner child work requires practicing self-advocacy and self-compassion. This involves advocating for our own needs and boundaries, even when it feels uncomfortable or challenging. By prioritizing self-compassion and self-care, we create a supportive inner environment in which our inner child feels valued and respected. Through self-advocacy and self-compassion, we empower ourselves to create a strong foundation of emotional support that nurtures our growth and healing on the journey of inner child work.

The Healing Power of Empathy

The healing power of empathy in inner child work cannot be overstated, as it serves as a bridge between our present-day selves and the wounded aspects of our inner child. Empathy involves the ability to understand and share the feelings of another, and in the context of inner child work, it allows us to extend compassion and understanding towards our own inner child. When we approach our inner child with empathy, we create a safe and nurturing space for healing to occur, as we validate and honor the emotions and experiences that have shaped our inner world.

Empathy also plays a crucial role in fostering self-compassion and acceptance in inner child work. By empathizing with the pain and suffering of our inner child, we cultivate a deeper sense of understanding and kindness towards ourselves. This compassionate response allows us to hold space for our own emotions and experiences with gentleness and care, fostering a sense of safety and trust that is essential for healing to unfold.

Furthermore, the healing power of empathy in inner child work extends beyond our relationship with ourselves to our interactions with others. As we cultivate empathy for our own inner child, we become more attuned to the emotions and experiences of those around us. This heightened sense of empathy allows us to connect more deeply with others, fostering greater compassion, understanding, and support in our relationships. Ultimately, the healing power of empathy in inner child work enables us to create a more empathetic and compassionate world, one in which healing and growth are possible for all.

Creating a Self-Compassionate Mindset

Creating a self-compassionate mindset is a transformative journey that begins with acknowledging and accepting our imperfections. In a world that often values perfection and achievement above all else, it can be easy to fall into the trap of self-criticism and self-judgment when we inevitably fall short of our own expectations. However, by acknowledging our imperfections with kindness and understanding, we can begin to cultivate a more compassionate relationship with ourselves. This involves recognizing that imperfection is a natural part of the human experience and that we are worthy of love and acceptance regardless of our flaws.

Central to creating a self-compassionate mindset is cultivating positive self-talk. Our internal dialogue has a profound impact on how we perceive ourselves and the world around us. By consciously choosing to speak to ourselves with kindness, encouragement, and positivity, we can shift our mindset from one of self-criticism to one of self-compassion. This involves challenging negative self-talk and replacing it with affirmations and words of self-encouragement. For example, instead of berating ourselves for making a mistake, we can acknowledge our efforts and remind ourselves that it's okay to be imperfect.

Another key aspect of creating a self-compassionate mindset is practicing mindfulness. Mindfulness involves paying attention to our thoughts, feelings, and sensations in the present moment without judgment. By cultivating present-moment awareness, we can observe our thoughts and emotions with curiosity and compassion, rather than getting caught up in self-critical or negative patterns of thinking. Mindfulness also allows us to develop greater self-awareness and insight into our own thought processes, empowering us to respond to ourselves and others with greater empathy and understanding.

Additionally, creating a self-compassionate mindset involves learning to treat ourselves with the same level of care and compassion that we would offer to a dear friend or loved one. This means prioritizing self-care and self-compassion in our daily lives, whether through engaging in activities that bring us joy and fulfillment, setting healthy boundaries, or practicing acts of self-kindness and self-love. By nurturing ourselves with care and compassion, we create a supportive inner environment in which we can flourish and grow.

Ultimately, creating a self-compassionate mindset is a journey of self-discovery and self-acceptance. It involves embracing our imperfections with kindness and understanding, cultivating positive self-talk, practicing mindfulness, and treating ourselves with care and compassion. By prioritizing self-compassion in our lives, we can cultivate a deeper sense of self-love, acceptance, and resilience, empowering ourselves to navigate life's challenges with grace and compassion.

Mindfulness and Present-Moment Awareness

In the realm of inner child work, mindfulness and present-moment awareness serve as invaluable tools for navigating the depths of our inner world with compassion and clarity. Mindfulness involves paying deliberate attention to the present moment, without judgment or attachment to thoughts, feelings, or sensations. This practice allows us to observe our inner experiences with curiosity and openness, creating space for self-discovery and healing to unfold. By cultivating present-moment awareness in inner child work, we can become more attuned to the needs and emotions of our inner child, offering comfort and support where it is needed most.

Practicing mindfulness in inner child work involves bringing a gentle and compassionate presence to our inner experiences, no matter how challenging or uncomfortable they may be. This means approaching our emotions, memories, and sensations with curiosity and non-judgment, allowing them to arise and pass away without resistance. By practicing mindfulness, we can develop a greater sense of self-awareness and self-compassion, as we learn to respond to our inner experiences with kindness and understanding. This mindful approach to inner child work allows us to create a safe and nurturing inner environment in which healing and growth can occur.

Furthermore, mindful self-compassion plays a vital role in inner child work, as it involves extending kindness and understanding towards ourselves in moments of difficulty or distress. By practicing mindful self-compassion, we offer ourselves the same level of care and compassion that we would offer to a dear friend or loved one. This practice involves acknowledging our own suffering with empathy and tenderness, and offering ourselves words of comfort and support. By cultivating mindful self-compassion in inner child work, we create a supportive inner environment in which our inner child feels seen, heard, and valued, paving the way for healing and transformation to occur.

Navigating Setbacks with Self-Love

Navigating setbacks with self-love in inner child work is an essential aspect of the healing journey, as it allows us to cultivate resilience and compassion in the face of adversity. Setbacks are a natural part of the healing process, and they can arise for various reasons, such as triggering events, unresolved emotions, or old patterns resurfacing. When setbacks occur, it's important to treat ourselves with kindness and understanding, rather than falling into self-criticism or defeatism. By embracing resilience and responding to setbacks with self-love, we can turn challenges into opportunities for growth and transformation.

One way to navigate setbacks with self-love in inner child work is to approach them with curiosity and openness. Rather than viewing setbacks as failures or obstacles, we can see them as opportunities for learning and self-discovery. By exploring the underlying causes of setbacks with compassion and non-judgment, we can gain insight into our inner world and uncover the deeper layers of our healing journey. This process allows us to cultivate greater self-awareness and resilience, empowering us to navigate setbacks with grace and resilience.

Furthermore, treating setbacks with kindness involves practicing self-compassion and self-care. Self-compassion involves offering ourselves the same level of care and understanding that we would offer to a dear friend or loved one. When setbacks occur, we can respond to ourselves with kindness and empathy, acknowledging our own suffering and offering ourselves words of comfort and support. Additionally, practicing self-care is essential for replenishing our energy reserves and nurturing our well-being during challenging times. Whether through engaging in activities that bring us joy and relaxation, seeking support from others, or simply taking time to rest and recharge, self-care allows us to nourish ourselves on a deep level and cultivate resilience in the face of setbacks.

Moreover, navigating setbacks with self-love in inner child work involves reframing our perspective and focusing on our progress rather than our setbacks. It's important to recognize that setbacks are not indicative of failure but rather a natural part of the healing journey. By acknowledging the progress we've made and celebrating our successes, no matter how small, we can cultivate a sense of gratitude and resilience that empowers us to persevere in the face of adversity. Through this lens of self-love and resilience, setbacks become opportunities for growth and transformation, allowing us to deepen our understanding of ourselves and our inner world with compassion and grace.

Journaling and Reflective Practices

Journaling and reflective practices play a vital role in inner child work, offering a powerful means of self-expression, exploration, and healing. Self-reflective journaling provides a safe and private space for individuals to explore their inner thoughts, feelings, and experiences. By putting pen to paper, we can delve deep into our subconscious minds, uncovering hidden patterns, beliefs, and emotions that may be influencing our lives. Through self-reflective journaling, we gain insight into our inner world and develop a greater understanding of ourselves, our motivations, and our relationships.

Gratitude journaling is another valuable practice in inner child work, as it helps to shift our focus from what is lacking in our lives to what we are grateful for. By cultivating an attitude of gratitude, we train our minds to notice and appreciate the positive aspects of our lives, no matter how small. This practice has been shown to have numerous benefits for mental and emotional well-being, including increased happiness, resilience, and overall life satisfaction. In the context of inner child work, gratitude journaling can help to reframe our perspective and foster a greater sense of self-love and acceptance.

Incorporating journaling and reflective practices into inner child work can take many forms, from free-form writing to structured prompts and exercises. Some individuals may find it helpful to set aside dedicated time each day or week for journaling, while others may prefer to jot down their thoughts and reflections as they arise throughout the day. The key is to find a journaling practice that feels authentic and supportive to you, allowing you to connect with your inner child and explore your emotions with honesty and compassion. Whether through self-reflective journaling, gratitude journaling, or a combination of both, journaling and reflective practices can be powerful tools for healing and growth in inner child work, helping us to navigate the complexities of our inner world with greater clarity, insight, and self-awareness.

Seeking Professional Support

Seeking professional support is a crucial aspect of inner child work, providing individuals with guidance, validation, and a safe space for exploration and healing. Therapeutic guidance from trained professionals, such as therapists, counselors, or psychologists, can offer invaluable support on the journey of inner child work. These professionals have the expertise and experience to help individuals navigate the complexities of their inner world, providing insights, tools, and techniques for healing and growth. Through therapy, individuals can explore their past experiences, uncovering the roots of their emotional wounds and developing strategies for healing and integration.

In addition to individual therapy, support groups can also be a valuable resource for those engaged in inner child work. Support groups offer a sense of community and belonging, allowing individuals to connect with others who may be on a similar healing journey. In these groups, individuals can share their experiences, offer support and encouragement to one another, and gain perspective and insights from the shared wisdom of the group. Support groups provide a safe and non-judgmental space for individuals to express themselves authentically and receive validation and understanding from others who have walked a similar path. Whether through therapeutic guidance or support groups, seeking professional support can provide invaluable assistance and encouragement on the journey of inner child work, helping individuals to heal, grow, and thrive.

Conclusion: The Gentle Symphony of Healing

In the orchestration of healing, emotional support and self-compassion form a gentle symphony that resonates with the deepest parts of the self. By embracing the kindness extended by others and cultivating self-compassion, individuals create a harmonious environment for the inner child to heal and thrive. As we weave emotional support and self-compassion into the tapestry of our healing journey, we discover that these tender mercies are not only vital companions but also powerful catalysts for transformation and resilience.

Chapter 6

Techniques for Inner Child Healing

A Comprehensive Guide to Healing Techniques: Nurturing Mind, Body, and Soul

Healing is a multi-faceted journey, and incorporating diverse techniques can foster profound transformation. This comprehensive guide explores various healing methods, each contributing to the holistic well-being of the individual. From journaling to meditation, creative expression to hypnosis, these techniques empower individuals to navigate the labyrinth of healing with intention and resilience.

1. Journaling for Self-Reflection:

Purpose: Journaling serves as a cathartic outlet for emotions and thoughts, providing a tangible space for self-reflection.

How to Practice:

- Daily Entries: Dedicate time each day to write about thoughts, feelings, and experiences.

- Prompted Journaling: Use prompts to explore specific aspects of healing or inner child work.

- Gratitude Journaling: Focus on positive aspects to foster a more optimistic mindset.

Benefits:

- Emotional Release

- Increased Self-Awareness

- Stress Reduction

2. Mindfulness Meditation:

Purpose: Mindfulness meditation cultivates present-moment awareness, allowing individuals to observe thoughts and emotions without judgment.

How to Practice:

- Breath Awareness: Focus on the breath, observing inhalations and exhalations.

- Body Scan: Scan through the body, paying attention to sensations without attachment.

- Guided Meditations: Use guided sessions led by experienced meditation teachers.

Benefits:

- Stress Reduction
- Improved Emotional Regulation
- Enhanced Mind-Body Connection

3. Creative Expression:

Purpose: Engaging in creative activities provides an expressive outlet for emotions, fostering healing through art, music, or writing.

How to Practice:

- Art Therapy: Create visual expressions of emotions through painting, drawing, or sculpting.
- Music Therapy: Use music as a means of emotional expression or relaxation.
- Writing as Therapy: Pen down narratives, poetry, or letters to explore emotions.

Benefits:

- Emotional Release
- Increased Self-Discovery
- Stress Reduction

4. Hypnosis and Guided Imagery:

Purpose: Hypnosis and guided imagery tap into the subconscious mind, allowing for exploration and reprogramming of thought patterns.

How to Practice:

- Guided Hypnosis Sessions: Use pre-recorded or live sessions with a qualified professional.

- Self-Hypnosis Techniques: Learn and practice self-hypnosis for autonomy.

- Guided Imagery: Visualize positive scenarios or explore inner landscapes for emotional healing.

Benefits:

- Reprogramming Negative Thought Patterns

- Stress Reduction

- Enhanced Relaxation

5. Yoga for Mind-Body Connection:

Purpose: Yoga combines physical postures, breathwork, and mindfulness to promote overall well-being and balance.

How to Practice:

- Asana Practice: Engage in physical postures to strengthen the body.

- Pranayama: Explore breathwork techniques for relaxation.
- Meditative Practices: Incorporate mindfulness into yoga sessions.

Benefits:

- Improved Flexibility and Strength
- Stress Reduction
- Mind-Body Connection

6. Therapeutic Writing and Narrative Therapy:

Purpose: Therapeutic writing and narrative therapy help individuals reconstruct their personal narratives, empowering them to reframe experiences.

How to Practice:

- Letter Writing: Address unresolved emotions by writing letters to oneself or others.
- Life Story Writing: Explore and reconstruct personal narratives.
- Future Scripting: Create positive narratives for future experiences.

Benefits:

- Empowerment through Storytelling

- Cognitive Restructuring

- Increased Self-Understanding

7. Energy Healing Practices:

Purpose: Energy healing methods, such as Reiki or Qi Gong, focus on balancing and harmonizing the body's energy centers.

How to Practice:

- Reiki Sessions: Receive energy healing from a certified practitioner.

- Qi Gong Exercises: Engage in gentle movements and breathwork.

- Chakra Balancing: Explore practices to align and balance energy centers.

Benefits:

- Stress Reduction

- Emotional Release

- Enhanced Energy Flow

8. Breathwork for Emotional Release:

Purpose: Conscious breathwork techniques facilitate emotional release and promote relaxation.

How to Practice:

- Deep Diaphragmatic Breathing: Focus on slow, deep breaths to activate the relaxation response.

- Pranayama Techniques: Explore yogic breathwork practices.

- Breath Awareness Meditation: Combine mindfulness with breath awareness.

Benefits:

- Stress Reduction

- Emotional Release

- Improved Oxygenation of the Body

9. Nature Therapy (Ecotherapy):

Purpose: Nature therapy involves connecting with the natural world to promote healing and well-being.

How to Practice:

- Forest Bathing: Immerse oneself in the sights, sounds, and smells of nature.

- Outdoor Meditation: Practice meditation in a natural setting.

- Nature Walks: Engage in mindful walks to connect with the environment.

Benefits:

- Stress Reduction

- Improved Mood

- Enhanced Connection with the Environment

Conclusion: Crafting Your Healing Journey:

The healing journey is unique to each individual, and the integration of various techniques offers a personalized and holistic approach. Combining these practices allows for a synergistic effect, addressing mind, body, and soul. As you embark on your healing journey, explore these techniques with curiosity and an open heart. Be patient, be kind to yourself, and embrace the transformative power that lies within the intentional practice of diverse healing modalities.

Real-life examples of successful healing journeys

Case Study 1: Mindful Transformation Through Meditation

Background:

Alex, a high-stress professional in his early 40s, grappled with chronic anxiety and difficulty managing work-related pressure. He decided to explore meditation as a tool for stress reduction and emotional well-being.

Healing Journey:

Alex began a mindfulness meditation practice, starting with short sessions and gradually increasing duration. He attended meditation classes and used guided meditation apps to deepen his practice.

Through meditation, he aimed to develop awareness of his thoughts and emotions, fostering a sense of calm and presence.

Success Indicators:

- Reduced Anxiety: Over time, Alex reported a significant reduction in anxiety levels, attributing it to the calming effects of regular meditation.

- Improved Focus and Productivity: Meditation enhanced his ability to stay focused on tasks, leading to increased productivity at work.

- Enhanced Emotional Regulation: Alex learned to observe his emotions without becoming overwhelmed, allowing for more measured responses to challenging situations.

Lesson Learned:

Alex's journey underscores the transformative impact of mindfulness meditation on stress reduction, emotional regulation, and overall well-being.

Case Study 2: Healing Trauma Through Therapeutic Writing

Background:

Emma, a survivor of childhood trauma, struggled with unresolved emotions and recurring nightmares. Seeking a therapeutic outlet, she turned to expressive writing as a means to process her experiences.

Healing Journey:

Emma began journaling regularly, documenting her thoughts, feelings, and memories related to the traumatic events. Guided by a trauma-informed therapist, she engaged in narrative therapy, gradually reconstructing her narrative to foster healing and understanding.

Success Indicators:

- Emotional Release: Writing provided a safe space for Emma to express and release deep-seated emotions associated with her trauma.

- Cognitive Restructuring: Through therapeutic writing, Emma challenged and reframed negative thought patterns, fostering a more positive and empowered self-perception.

- Decreased Nightmares: Emma reported a decrease in the frequency and intensity of nightmares as she processed and externalized her traumatic experiences.

Lesson Learned:

Emma's journey illustrates the therapeutic potential of expressive writing in processing trauma, reframing narratives, and promoting emotional healing.

Case Study 3: Hypnosis for Overcoming Phobias

Background:

John, in his early 30s, struggled with a severe phobia that significantly impacted his daily life. Seeking a non-traditional approach, he decided to explore hypnosis as a means to address and overcome his fear.

Healing Journey:

Under the guidance of a certified hypnotherapist, John underwent several hypnosis sessions tailored to address the root causes of his phobia. The sessions focused on reprogramming his subconscious responses and fostering a sense of safety.

Success Indicators:

- Phobia Reduction: John experienced a significant reduction in the intensity of his phobia, allowing him to engage in activities he previously avoided.

- Increased Confidence: Hypnosis contributed to an improvement in John's overall confidence and sense of self-efficacy.

- Behavioral Shifts: Over time, John demonstrated a willingness to confront and gradually overcome situations associated with his phobia.

Lesson Learned:

John's success with hypnosis highlights its potential as a complementary therapeutic tool for addressing specific fears and phobias, demonstrating the role of subconscious reprogramming in behavioral change.

These real-life examples demonstrate the diverse ways in which meditation, therapeutic writing, and hypnosis can contribute to successful healing journeys. Each case underscores the importance of individualized approaches and the transformative power of these techniques in promoting emotional well-being and personal growth.

Chapter 7
Overcoming Resistance and Obstacles

Common challenges in inner child work

Navigating Murky Waters: Common Challenges in Inner Child Work

Embarking on the journey of inner child work is a transformative endeavor, but it is not without its share of challenges. This chapter delves into the common hurdles individuals may encounter as they navigate the delicate terrain of reconnecting with and healing their inner child. Acknowledging and understanding these challenges is essential for fostering resilience and navigating the healing process with greater insight.

Resurfacing Painful Memories

Engaging in inner child work presents a challenge as it often entails revisiting painful memories from the past, which can evoke intense emotions and be emotionally overwhelming. To navigate this challenge effectively, it is crucial to establish a strong foundation of self-care, mindfulness, and seeking professional support. Practicing self-care techniques such as setting boundaries, engaging in activities that bring comfort and joy, and prioritizing rest and relaxation can help in creating a safe space for emotional exploration.

Additionally, cultivating mindfulness through practices like meditation and journaling can aid in staying present with difficult emotions and thoughts as they arise. Seeking support from a therapist or counselor who specializes in inner child work can provide guidance, validation, and a compassionate presence throughout the healing journey. Together, these strategies can offer a safe container for processing and managing the resurfacing of difficult memories, facilitating healing and growth in inner child work.

Resistance and Defense Mechanisms

Engaging in inner child work often encounters the challenge of the inner child's resistance, which is often guarded by defense mechanisms. These defense mechanisms, formed as a means of self-protection in response to past traumas, can manifest as avoidance or denial of the healing process. The inner child may resist delving into painful memories or emotions, fearing further hurt or vulnerability. This resistance can create barriers to healing, hindering the individual's progress in their inner child work.

Handling this setback requires patience and gentle persistence. Building a trusting relationship with the inner child takes time and consistent efforts. It's essential to approach the inner child with compassion and understanding, acknowledging their fears and respecting their boundaries. Mindfulness practices can be particularly helpful in navigating resistance, as they allow individuals to observe their thoughts and emotions without judgment. By cultivating mindfulness, individuals can develop a deeper awareness of their inner dynamics, allowing them to gently address resistance and foster a sense of safety and trust within themselves.

As individuals continue their inner child work journey, they may gradually uncover the underlying reasons for the inner child's resistance and begin to address them with compassion and empathy. Through consistent practice and self-reflection, individuals can gradually break down the barriers of resistance and create space for healing and growth. By embracing patience, persistence, and mindfulness, individuals can navigate the challenge of inner child resistance and foster a nurturing environment for their inner child's healing journey.

Fear of Vulnerability

Opening up to vulnerability is a significant challenge in inner child work, particularly for individuals who have developed emotional armor as a means of self-protection. For many, the idea of exposing their true emotions and experiences can be intimidating, as it requires them to let go of the defenses they have built over time. This emotional armor serves as a barrier against pain and hurt, but it also prevents individuals from fully connecting with their inner child and experiencing authentic healing.

Addressing this difficulty involves creating a secure and non-judgmental environment where individuals feel safe to explore their vulnerability. Establishing trust and rapport with oneself and any support systems is crucial. Encouraging self-compassion and recognizing the courage it takes to be vulnerable can help counteract fears and uncertainties. By fostering a compassionate and understanding mindset, individuals can begin to dismantle their emotional armor and allow themselves to be more open and authentic in their inner child work.

Practicing self-compassion involves treating oneself with kindness and understanding, particularly during moments of vulnerability and discomfort. It's essential to remind oneself that vulnerability is a strength, not a weakness, and that embracing one's true emotions is an integral part of the healing journey. By reframing vulnerability as a courageous act of self-discovery and growth, individuals can overcome their fears and begin to cultivate a deeper connection with their inner child. Through patience, self-compassion, and a supportive environment, individuals can navigate the challenge of opening up to vulnerability and experience profound healing and transformation in their inner child work.

Inner Critic and Self-Judgment

One of the significant challenges individuals encounter during inner child work is the presence of the inner critic, a voice shaped by critical experiences from childhood. This inner critic often becomes amplified during the process of inner child work, leading to heightened self-judgment and undermining the individual's progress. The inner critic may berate individuals for their perceived shortcomings or mistakes, instilling feelings of inadequacy and self-doubt.

Managing this adversity requires a deliberate effort to develop a compassionate inner dialogue. It's essential for individuals to recognize the origins of their inner critic and understand that it stems from past experiences and conditioning. By acknowledging the root cause of the inner critic's harshness, individuals can begin to cultivate self-compassion and respond to themselves with greater kindness and understanding.

Consciously replacing negative self-talk with affirming language is a key aspect of tackling this problem posed by the inner critic. Individuals can practice affirmations and positive self-statements to counteract the damaging effects of the inner critic's voice. By affirming their worth, strengths, and inherent value, individuals can gradually diminish the power of the inner critic and create a more nurturing inner environment conducive to healing and growth.

In addition to affirmations, mindfulness practices can also be beneficial in navigating the challenge of the inner critic. By practicing mindfulness, individuals can observe their thoughts and emotions without attachment or judgment, allowing them to cultivate a sense of inner calm and detachment from the critical voice. Through consistent practice and self-awareness, individuals can learn to differentiate between the voice of their inner critic and their authentic self, empowering them to reclaim control over their inner narrative and foster greater self-compassion in their inner child work.

Impatience and Desire for Quick Fixes

Engaging in inner child work often presents the challenge of impatience, as individuals may yearn for immediate results and tangible progress. However, inner child work is a gradual process that requires time, dedication,

and patience. Frustration can arise when individuals expect quick fixes or significant breakthroughs without fully acknowledging the complexities of their inner healing journey.

Dealing with this issue involves cultivating patience and embracing the journey as a continual process of self-discovery and growth. It's essential for individuals to set realistic expectations and understand that inner child work unfolds at its own pace. By reframing impatience as an opportunity for learning and self-reflection, individuals can adopt a more sustainable approach to their healing journey. Celebrating small milestones along the way, no matter how minor they may seem, can provide encouragement and motivation to continue moving forward on the path towards healing and wholeness.

Reparenting Challenges

Reparenting in inner child work presents a challenge for individuals who lacked nurturing parental figures during childhood. Acting as a compassionate and supportive inner parent to the wounded inner child may feel unfamiliar or even daunting. The absence of positive parental role models in childhood can leave individuals without a reference point for nurturing behaviors, making it challenging to embody the role of a loving caregiver to their inner child.

Confronting this dilemma involves seeking guidance from therapists and utilizing various techniques to cultivate reparenting skills. Therapists specializing in inner child work can offer valuable insights and support, helping individuals develop strategies to connect with their inner child in a nurturing and compassionate manner. Visualization techniques, such as imagining oneself as a loving parent comforting and nurturing the inner child, can also be helpful in fostering a sense of parental care and support.

Additionally, practicing self-compassion is essential in reparenting, as individuals learn to treat themselves with the same kindness and understanding they would offer to a beloved child. Reparenting is an ongoing process that evolves with time, patience, and practice, ultimately leading to greater healing and self-acceptance.

Integration of New Self-Perceptions

Embracing evolving self-perceptions and shedding old, limiting beliefs is a significant challenge in inner child work. As individuals delve into their past experiences and explore the root causes of their beliefs and behaviors, they may encounter resistance and discomfort. Letting go of familiar but restrictive narratives about oneself can feel disorienting, as it requires stepping into uncharted territory and embracing a new sense of identity and self-worth.

Addressing this difficulty involves implementing various strategies to facilitate the integration of healthier self-perceptions. Consistent affirmation is key, as individuals consciously reaffirm positive qualities and strengths, counteracting the influence of old, limiting beliefs. Engaging in cognitive restructuring techniques helps individuals challenge and reframe negative thought patterns, allowing them to adopt more empowering perspectives about themselves and their capabilities. Self-reflection plays a vital role in the process, as individuals examine their beliefs and behaviors with curiosity and openness, seeking to understand how they may have been shaped by past experiences.

Seeking support from therapy or support groups can be invaluable in navigating the challenge of embracing evolving self-perceptions. Therapists specializing in inner child work can provide guidance, validation, and insight, helping individuals explore and process their emotions and experiences in a safe and supportive environment. Support groups offer the opportunity to connect with others who are on similar journeys, providing validation, encouragement, and a sense of community. Together, these strategies and sources of support contribute to the ongoing process of inner healing and transformation, empowering individuals to embrace their evolving self-perceptions with courage and resilience.

Fear of Change

Inner child work is often a journey of profound transformation, leading to shifts in behavior and perspectives that can be both liberating and daunting. As individuals delve into their inner selves and confront past wounds and traumas, they may uncover deeply ingrained patterns of behavior and belief systems that no longer serve them. However, embracing these transformative changes can be met with resistance, as the fear of the unknown looms large. The prospect of stepping into uncharted territory and relinquishing familiar but limiting ways of being can evoke feelings of apprehension and uncertainty.

Overcoming this obstacle requires a gentle and phased approach to change, allowing individuals to ease into the process of transformation at their own pace. Gradual steps and incremental adjustments help individuals acclimate to new behaviors and perspectives without overwhelming themselves. By breaking down the process into manageable stages, individuals can build confidence and resilience as they navigate the uncertainties of inner child work.

Additionally, having a supportive network of friends, family, or therapists can provide invaluable encouragement and guidance along the way. Knowing that they are not alone in their journey can offer reassurance and strength to individuals facing resistance and uncertainty.

Recognizing and celebrating positive changes is another essential aspect of navigating the challenge of transformative inner child work. By acknowledging the progress they have made and honoring the growth they have experienced, individuals reinforce a sense of empowerment and agency in their healing journey. Celebrating milestones, no matter how small, serves as a reminder of their resilience and determination to create positive change in their lives. With patience, support, and self-compassion, individuals can navigate the challenges of inner child work and embrace the transformative journey with courage and grace.

Conclusion: Embracing Challenges as Catalysts for Growth

While inner child work may present challenges, each obstacle encountered is an opportunity for growth and healing. Understanding that the journey is unique for every individual and that challenges are natural aspects of the process empowers individuals to navigate the murky waters with resilience and self-compassion. In facing these challenges head-on, individuals embark on a path toward reclaiming their authenticity and fostering profound inner healing.

Strategies for Overcoming Resistance and Fear

Overcoming resistance and fear in inner child work requires a compassionate and patient approach. Here are strategies to navigate common challenges and foster a more supportive inner environment.

Establish a Foundation of Self-Care

Establishing a foundation of self-care is paramount in inner child work, providing individuals with the necessary support and resilience to navigate their healing journey. Self-care encompasses various practices aimed at nurturing one's physical, emotional, and mental well-being. Prioritizing self-care involves tuning into one's needs and taking proactive steps to meet them, fostering a sense of self-compassion and self-respect.

At its core, self-care involves recognizing and honoring one's boundaries, setting aside time for activities that bring joy and relaxation, and prioritizing rest and rejuvenation. Engaging in activities such as mindfulness meditation, yoga, journaling, or spending time in nature can help individuals cultivate a deeper sense of self-awareness and inner peace. By incorporating self-care practices into their daily routine, individuals create a supportive framework that fosters emotional resilience and promotes overall well-being.

In the context of inner child work, self-care takes on added significance as individuals navigate the complexities of their inner world and confront past traumas. Establishing a foundation of self-care serves as a vital anchor, providing individuals with the strength and stability to process difficult emotions and experiences. By prioritizing self-care, individuals demonstrate a commitment to their healing journey and cultivate a nurturing environment that supports their inner child's growth and transformation.

Mindfulness and Grounding Techniques

Mindfulness and grounding techniques play a crucial role in inner child work, offering individuals powerful tools to cultivate self-awareness and presence in the present moment. Mindfulness involves intentionally paying attention to one's thoughts, feelings, and bodily sensations without judgment, while grounding techniques help individuals connect with the here and now, anchoring themselves in the present reality. Together, these practices provide a foundation for inner exploration and healing.

One of the fundamental aspects of mindfulness is the practice of observing thoughts and emotions with curiosity and compassion. By cultivating a non-judgmental attitude towards their inner experiences, individuals create a safe space for their inner child to express itself freely. Through mindfulness, individuals learn to acknowledge and validate their emotions without becoming overwhelmed by them, fostering a sense of inner peace and acceptance.

Grounding techniques complement mindfulness practices by helping individuals anchor themselves in the present moment and regulate their emotions. These techniques often involve engaging the senses to bring attention to the here and now, such as focusing on the breath, noticing the sensations of the body, or observing the sights, sounds, and smells in the environment. By grounding themselves in the present reality, individuals can soothe their nervous system and alleviate symptoms of anxiety or distress, creating a sense of stability and safety within.

In the context of inner child work, mindfulness and grounding techniques serve as invaluable resources for navigating the complexities of past trauma and emotional wounds. When confronted with challenging memories or overwhelming emotions, individuals can turn to these practices to ground themselves in the present moment and cultivate a sense of inner resilience. By developing a regular mindfulness practice and incorporating grounding techniques into their daily routine, individuals empower themselves to engage with their inner child with clarity, compassion, and courage. Through the power of mindfulness and grounding, individuals can embark on a journey of self-discovery and healing, reclaiming wholeness and authenticity in their lives.

Progressive Exposure to Painful Memories

Progressive exposure to painful memories is a pivotal aspect of inner child work, allowing individuals to gradually confront and process past traumas in a safe and supportive environment. This approach involves breaking down overwhelming memories or experiences into smaller, more manageable components, which are explored and addressed at a pace that feels comfortable for the individual. By progressively exposing themselves to painful memories, individuals can gradually build resilience and develop coping strategies to navigate difficult emotions.

The process of progressive exposure begins with gentle exploration of less distressing memories before gradually moving towards more challenging ones. This gradual approach helps individuals build trust in themselves and their ability to navigate their emotions, fostering a sense of empowerment and agency in their healing journey. Through each step of exposure, individuals learn to tolerate discomfort and uncertainty, ultimately gaining a deeper understanding of themselves and their past experiences.

While progressive exposure to painful memories can evoke strong emotions and discomfort, it also provides an opportunity for profound healing and transformation. By facing their past traumas with courage and compassion, individuals can release the grip of unresolved pain and reclaim control over their lives. With the support of a therapist or trusted guide, individuals can navigate the complexities of progressive exposure, paving the way for profound healing and inner liberation.

Journaling for Self-Reflection

Journaling for self-reflection is a powerful tool in the practice of inner child work, offering individuals a safe and private space to explore their thoughts, feelings, and experiences. Through the act of writing, individuals can gain insight into their inner world, uncovering patterns, beliefs, and emotions that may be deeply rooted in their past. Journaling allows individuals to express themselves freely, without fear of judgment or criticism, facilitating a process of self-discovery and healing.

One of the key benefits of journaling for self-reflection is its ability to provide clarity and perspective on one's inner experiences. By putting pen to paper, individuals can externalize their thoughts and emotions, making them tangible and easier to understand. Journaling allows individuals to untangle complex emotions and gain a deeper understanding of their inner landscape, enabling them to identify areas of growth and areas in need of healing.

In the context of inner child work, journaling serves as a valuable tool for processing past traumas and exploring the impact of childhood experiences on one's present-day life. Through journaling, individuals can delve into memories, emotions, and beliefs associated with their inner child, gaining insight into how past wounds continue to shape their thoughts, behaviors, and relationships. By documenting their inner journey in a journal, individuals can track their progress, celebrate milestones, and cultivate a sense of empowerment and agency in their healing process.

Inner Dialogue and Affirmations

Inner dialogue and affirmations are essential components of inner child work, offering individuals powerful tools to cultivate self-compassion, self-awareness, and self-empowerment.

Inner dialogue involves the ongoing conversation individuals have with themselves, encompassing their thoughts, beliefs, and self-perceptions. By cultivating a compassionate and supportive inner dialogue, individuals can challenge negative self-talk and cultivate a more nurturing and empowering relationship with themselves.

Affirmations are positive statements that individuals repeat to themselves regularly, with the intention of reprogramming their subconscious mind and reinforcing positive beliefs about themselves and their abilities. Affirmations serve as powerful tools for inner child work, helping individuals counteract negative self-talk and internalized beliefs that may have originated from childhood experiences. By consciously choosing and repeating affirmations that reflect their inherent worth, strength, and resilience, individuals can foster a sense of self-empowerment and self-worth.

In the context of inner child work, inner dialogue and affirmations play a crucial role in supporting individuals as they navigate their healing journey. Through mindful awareness of their inner dialogue, individuals can identify and challenge negative self-talk and limiting beliefs that may be rooted in past traumas or childhood experiences. By replacing these negative narratives with affirming and empowering statements, individuals can reframe their self-perceptions and cultivate a more positive and compassionate relationship with themselves. Inner dialogue and affirmations serve as powerful tools for nurturing the inner child, fostering a sense of safety, acceptance, and self-love that is essential for healing and growth.

Therapeutic Support

Seeking guidance from a therapist experienced in inner child work is a strategic step towards fostering healing and growth. With the expertise of a trained professional, individuals can embark on their inner child journey with support and guidance tailored to their unique needs. Therapists specialized in this area understand the complexities of childhood trauma and the intricacies of inner healing, providing a safe and nurturing environment for individuals to explore their inner world.

Implementing regular therapy sessions offers individuals a structured space to delve into their inner child work. Through consistent sessions, individuals can explore challenges, confront resistance, and develop coping strategies to navigate their healing journey. Therapists act as compassionate guides, offering valuable insights and tools to help individuals unravel past wounds and cultivate resilience. With the support of a therapist, individuals can gradually peel back the layers of their inner selves, gaining clarity and understanding along the way.

Therapists experienced in inner child work play a crucial role in helping individuals navigate resistance and overcome obstacles on their path to healing. By providing compassionate support and expert guidance, therapists empower individuals to confront their inner demons and reclaim their sense of self. Through the collaborative effort of therapist and client, individuals can embark on a transformative journey of self-discovery and healing, ultimately finding peace and wholeness within themselves.

Visualization and Reparenting Techniques

Utilizing visualization as a strategy in inner child work offers individuals a powerful tool for establishing a secure inner parent and reparenting the wounded inner child. Through visualization exercises, individuals can tap into their imagination to create a nurturing figure that embodies the qualities of a compassionate and supportive caregiver. This inner parent serves as a source of comfort and guidance, offering the inner child the care and understanding it may have lacked in childhood.

In implementing visualization techniques, individuals can imagine the presence of their inner parent during moments of distress or vulnerability. By visualizing this nurturing figure, individuals can evoke feelings of safety and security, providing a sense of reassurance and stability during challenging times. Engaging in reparenting exercises further solidifies the bond between the inner parent and inner child, as individuals practice offering themselves the care and compassion they may have yearned for in their formative years.

During reparenting exercises, individuals can actively participate in providing the care and understanding that their inner child needs. This may involve engaging in self-soothing activities, practicing self-compassion, or offering comforting affirmations to the inner child. By embodying the role of the nurturing caregiver, individuals can heal past wounds and cultivate a deeper sense of self-love and acceptance. Through consistent practice, reparenting exercises enable individuals to rewrite old narratives and create new, empowering experiences for their inner child.

Ultimately, visualization and reparenting techniques in inner child work allow individuals to establish a nurturing inner environment that supports healing and growth. By harnessing the power of imagination and self-compassion, individuals can cultivate a secure attachment to their inner parent, fostering a sense of safety and belonging within themselves. Through these transformative practices, individuals can embark on a journey of self-discovery and inner healing, reclaiming their inherent worth and embracing their true essence.

Celebrate Small Wins

In the realm of inner child work, acknowledging and celebrating progress, no matter how small, serves as a powerful strategy for nurturing healing and growth. By recognizing the incremental steps taken on the journey towards healing, individuals can cultivate a sense of accomplishment and momentum in their inner work. This strategy emphasizes the importance of valuing each step forward, no matter how minor it may seem, as it contributes to the overall progress and transformation.

In implementing this strategy, individuals can set realistic goals that align with their healing journey and personal growth aspirations. These goals provide clear milestones to strive towards, offering direction and focus in the inner child work process. By breaking down larger objectives into smaller, attainable steps, individuals can create achievable targets that are within reach. As individuals progress towards these goals, it's essential to pause and reflect on the achievements made along the way, no matter how modest they may appear.

Celebrating milestones in inner child work fosters a positive mindset and reinforces the idea that progress is being made. Whether it's acknowledging a breakthrough in therapy, practicing self-care, or confronting a fear rooted in childhood trauma, each milestone represents a significant achievement in the journey towards healing. By taking the time to celebrate these moments, individuals can cultivate a sense of pride and self-worth, affirming their capacity for growth and resilience. Through the consistent acknowledgment and celebration of progress, individuals can maintain motivation and momentum in their inner child work, propelling them towards greater healing and transformation.

Community and Support Groups

In the realm of inner child work, connecting with others who are on a similar healing journey serves as a powerful strategy for fostering support, validation, and encouragement. By reaching out to individuals who share similar experiences and challenges, individuals can cultivate a sense of belonging and community in their healing process. This strategy emphasizes the importance of peer support in navigating the complexities of inner child work and reinforces the understanding that one is not alone in their struggles.

In implementing this strategy, individuals can actively seek out support groups or communities where they can connect with others who are undergoing similar healing journeys. These groups provide a safe and non-judgmental space for individuals to share their experiences, seek guidance, and offer support to one another. Through open and honest communication, individuals can find validation for their feelings and experiences, as well as gain valuable insights and perspectives from others who have walked a similar path.

Peer support in inner child work offers a unique form of validation and understanding that can be instrumental in the healing process. By hearing the stories of others and witnessing their progress, individuals can feel encouraged and inspired to continue their own journey of healing and growth. Additionally, the sense of camaraderie and solidarity that comes from connecting with others who are on a similar path can provide a source of strength and resilience during challenging times. Through the mutual exchange of support and empathy, individuals can find solace in knowing that they are not alone in their struggles and that healing is possible with the support of others.

Embrace Fear as a Catalyst for Growth

In the realm of inner child work, reframing fear as an integral part of the healing process serves as a transformative strategy for embracing change and fostering personal growth. Rather than viewing fear as an obstacle to be avoided, individuals can recognize it as a natural response to the profound shifts occurring within themselves. This strategy emphasizes the importance of understanding fear as a sign of progress and transformation, rather than a hindrance to healing.

In implementing this strategy, individuals can begin by acknowledging that fear is a common and natural response to change and growth. By recognizing fear as a normal part of the healing journey, individuals can normalize their experiences and reduce feelings of shame or inadequacy surrounding their fears. Embracing fear as a companion on the path to healing allows individuals to cultivate a deeper sense of self-awareness and resilience in the face of challenges.

By reframing fear as an opportunity for profound personal development, individuals can harness its energy to propel them forward in their healing journey. Rather than allowing fear to hold them back, individuals can view it as a catalyst for growth and transformation. Embracing fear with courage and openness enables individuals to confront their innermost fears and insecurities, ultimately leading to greater self-discovery and empowerment. Through this reframing process, individuals can unlock new levels of healing and liberation, embracing fear as an integral part of their journey towards wholeness and self-acceptance.

Conclusion: A Compassionate Journey of Self-Discovery

Overcoming resistance and fear in inner child work is a gradual and ongoing process. By incorporating these strategies, individuals can foster a compassionate and supportive inner environment, allowing for the gradual release of resistance and fear. Remember, the journey is unique for each person, and progress is made one step at a time.

Patience, self-compassion, and a commitment to healing are key elements in navigating the challenges of inner child work.

Maintaining motivation and dealing with setbacks

Maintaining motivation and navigating setbacks in inner child work is crucial for sustained healing. Here are strategies to help individuals stay motivated and resilient, even in the face of challenges and setback.:

Cultivate Self-Compassion

In the realm of inner child work, cultivating a compassionate mindset towards oneself is a fundamental strategy for fostering self-love and healing. This strategy emphasizes the importance of extending kindness and understanding to oneself, especially during moments of setbacks or challenges. By developing a compassionate mindset, individuals can nurture a deeper sense of self-acceptance and resilience in their healing journey.

Implementing this strategy involves acknowledging that setbacks are a natural part of the healing process. Rather than viewing setbacks as failures or signs of inadequacy, individuals can recognize them as opportunities for growth and learning. By embracing setbacks with compassion and acceptance, individuals can navigate through difficult times with greater ease and grace. This involves treating oneself with the same level of kindness and understanding that one would offer to a friend facing similar challenges, fostering a sense of self-compassion and inner peace.

By adopting a compassionate mindset towards oneself, individuals can cultivate a supportive and nurturing inner environment conducive to healing. This involves practicing self-compassion, self-forgiveness, and self-care on a daily basis. Through gentle and loving self-talk, individuals can soothe their inner wounds and build resilience in the face of adversity. By prioritizing self-compassion and understanding, individuals can foster a deeper sense of self-worth and acceptance, ultimately leading to greater healing and wholeness in their lives.

Set Realistic Expectations

In the realm of inner child work, establishing achievable goals and milestones is a foundational strategy for fostering progress and growth. This approach emphasizes the importance of breaking down the journey of inner healing into manageable steps, allowing individuals to navigate their path with clarity and purpose. By setting specific goals and milestones, individuals can create a roadmap for their inner child work, enabling them to track their progress and celebrate their achievements along the way.

In implementing this strategy, individuals can begin by breaking down their inner child work into smaller, more manageable tasks or objectives. This might involve identifying specific areas of healing or growth that they wish to focus on, such as overcoming past trauma, building self-esteem, or improving emotional regulation. By breaking these larger goals into smaller, actionable steps, individuals can create a clear and achievable plan for their inner healing journey.

Setting realistic expectations is another crucial aspect of implementing this strategy. By acknowledging the limitations of time, energy, and resources, individuals can avoid feeling overwhelmed by the enormity of their inner child work. Instead of expecting immediate or miraculous results, individuals can recognize that healing is a gradual and ongoing process that unfolds over time. By setting realistic expectations, individuals can reduce the likelihood of setbacks becoming perceived failures and maintain a sense of motivation and resilience in their inner healing journey.

Learn from Setbacks

In the context of inner child work, viewing setbacks as opportunities for learning and growth is a transformative strategy that empowers individuals to navigate challenges with resilience and self-awareness. Rather than perceiving setbacks as failures or obstacles, this approach encourages individuals to reframe them as valuable learning experiences that contribute to their overall healing journey. By adopting this mindset, individuals can cultivate a sense of curiosity and openness towards setbacks, recognizing them as opportunities for deeper self-discovery and personal development.

Implementing this strategy involves a process of reflection and analysis to glean insights from setbacks and transform them into valuable learning opportunities. Individuals can begin by examining the circumstances surrounding the setback, identifying triggers, and recognizing any patterns or recurring themes. This self-exploration enables individuals to gain a deeper understanding of the underlying factors contributing to the setback and identify areas for growth and improvement in their inner child work.

Once setbacks have been analyzed and understood, individuals can then extract valuable lessons and insights from the experience. By reflecting on what went wrong and what could have been done differently, individuals can identify areas for adjustment and refinement in their inner child work strategy. This process of self-reflection and learning equips individuals with valuable information and tools for navigating future challenges with greater insight and resilience, ultimately empowering them to continue their journey of inner healing and growth.

Celebrate Small Victories

In the realm of inner child work, acknowledging and celebrating even the smallest achievements is a powerful strategy for fostering motivation and resilience on the healing journey. This approach emphasizes the importance of recognizing and honoring progress, no matter how minor it may seem. By shifting the focus towards celebrating small victories, individuals can cultivate a positive mindset and reinforce their commitment to inner healing and growth.

Implementing this strategy involves regularly reflecting on one's progress and achievements, no matter how small or seemingly insignificant they may be. Whether it's overcoming a fear, expressing an emotion, or setting a healthy boundary, taking the time to acknowledge these achievements is crucial for building confidence and self-esteem. By consciously pausing to recognize and celebrate these moments of progress, individuals can boost their motivation and reinforce the positive aspects of their healing journey.

Celebrating small victories not only boosts motivation but also reinforces the resilience and perseverance needed to overcome challenges along the way. By acknowledging how far they've come and the progress they've made, individuals can build a sense of momentum and confidence in their ability to navigate the ups and downs of inner child work. This process of celebration serves as a reminder that every step forward, no matter how small, is a testament to one's strength and determination.

Moreover, celebrating small achievements creates a ripple effect of positivity and empowerment throughout the inner child work journey. By consciously focusing on the positive aspects of their progress, individuals can cultivate a sense of gratitude and appreciation for their inner resilience and growth. This sense of celebration not only enhances motivation but also fosters a deeper sense of self-awareness and self-compassion, ultimately contributing to a more fulfilling and rewarding healing journey.

In essence, acknowledging and celebrating even the smallest achievements is a transformative practice that infuses the inner child work journey with positivity, resilience, and empowerment. By embracing this strategy, individuals can cultivate a sense of joy and fulfillment in their progress, reaffirming their commitment to inner healing and growth with each small victory celebrated along the way.

Utilize Support Systems

In the landscape of inner child work, leveraging the support of friends, family, or a therapist is a crucial strategy that can significantly enhance the healing journey. This approach emphasizes the importance of seeking support from trusted individuals who can offer encouragement, validation, and understanding along the way. By opening up and sharing experiences with those who care about us, we create a supportive network that serves as a source of strength and comfort during challenging times.

Implementing this strategy involves reaching out to friends, family members, or a therapist who can provide a safe space for expression and exploration. These trusted individuals can offer empathy, compassion, and valuable insights that help us navigate the complexities of our inner world. Whether it's discussing difficult emotions, processing past traumas, or seeking guidance on coping strategies, having a supportive network ensures that we are not alone in our journey of inner healing and growth.

Moreover, the support of friends, family, or a therapist can provide a sense of validation and affirmation that is essential for healing. When we share our experiences with others who understand and empathize with our struggles, we feel seen, heard, and valued. This validation helps to counteract feelings of isolation and self-doubt, fostering a sense of connection and belonging that is vital for our well-being. By leaning on our support network, we can navigate the ups and downs of inner child work with greater resilience and confidence, knowing that we have people who care about us by our side.

Revisit Coping Strategies

In the realm of inner child work, reassessing and strengthening coping mechanisms is a vital strategy for navigating challenges and setbacks along the healing journey. This approach emphasizes the importance of identifying effective coping strategies that help individuals cope with difficult emotions, triggers, and memories that may arise during the inner child work process. By proactively evaluating and strengthening these coping mechanisms, individuals can enhance their resilience and ability to manage stressors effectively.

Implementing this strategy involves taking stock of existing coping mechanisms and identifying those that have proven to be most helpful in times of distress. Whether it's practicing mindfulness, journaling, engaging in creative activities, or seeking support from loved ones, individuals can leverage a variety of tools to navigate setbacks and challenges with greater ease. By recognizing the effectiveness of these coping strategies, individuals can cultivate a sense of empowerment and agency in managing their emotional well-being.

Furthermore, actively utilizing these coping mechanisms during setbacks is essential for maintaining emotional balance and stability throughout the inner child work process. When faced with difficult emotions or triggers, individuals can turn to their established coping strategies as a source of comfort and support. Whether it's taking a few moments to practice mindfulness, writing in a journal to process emotions, or engaging in activities that bring joy and relaxation, these coping mechanisms serve as valuable resources for self-care and emotional regulation. By incorporating these practices into their daily routine, individuals can strengthen their resilience and build a solid foundation for continued growth and healing on their inner child work journey.

Visualize Long-Term Goals

In the context of inner child work, maintaining a long-term vision is a foundational strategy that provides individuals with clarity, purpose, and motivation throughout their healing journey. This approach emphasizes the importance of visualizing the desired outcome of inner child work, keeping sight of the overarching goals, and staying committed to the transformative process. By maintaining a long-term perspective, individuals can navigate challenges, setbacks, and obstacles with resilience and determination, knowing that their efforts are contributing to profound inner healing and growth.

Implementing this strategy involves engaging in visualization techniques that allow individuals to vividly imagine the desired outcomes of their inner child work. By visualizing a future where they have healed past wounds, developed healthy coping mechanisms, and cultivated a sense of self-love and acceptance, individuals can reinforce their motivation and commitment to the journey. Additionally, reconnecting with the initial motivation that prompted them to embark on the inner child work journey serves as a powerful reminder of the transformative potential inherent in the process. Whether it's seeking relief from emotional pain, improving relationships, or achieving greater self-awareness, individuals can reaffirm their dedication to inner healing by revisiting their underlying motivations.

Furthermore, keeping the long-term vision in mind provides individuals with a sense of direction and purpose, guiding their actions and decisions along the way. By focusing on the ultimate goals of inner child work, individuals can stay aligned with their values, priorities, and aspirations, even when faced with challenges or obstacles. This clarity of purpose helps individuals maintain momentum and resilience, empowering them to persevere through difficult times and stay committed to their healing journey. Ultimately, by keeping the long-term vision in mind, individuals can harness the transformative power of inner child work to create profound and lasting changes in their lives.

.

Break the Stigma of Perfection

In the realm of inner child work, embracing imperfections and accepting the non-linear nature of healing is a foundational strategy that fosters resilience, self-compassion, and growth. This approach encourages individuals to challenge the pervasive notion of perfection and instead embrace the inherent messiness and complexity of the healing journey. By acknowledging that healing is not a linear path and that setbacks are a natural part of the process, individuals can cultivate a more compassionate and forgiving attitude towards themselves and their progress.

Implementing this strategy involves actively challenging the notion of perfection and reframing setbacks as opportunities for learning and growth. Rather than viewing setbacks as failures or evidence of inadequacy, individuals can recognize them as integral parts of the journey towards healing. Each setback presents an opportunity to gain valuable insights, deepen self-awareness, and refine coping strategies. By reframing setbacks in this way, individuals can shift their perspective from one of self-criticism to one of self-compassion and empowerment.

Moreover, embracing imperfections and accepting the non-linear nature of healing allows individuals to appreciate the progress they have made, even in the face of setbacks. Rather than focusing solely on the end goal, individuals can celebrate the small victories and milestones along the way. Each step taken, regardless of setbacks or detours, contributes to overall progress and growth. By acknowledging and honoring their efforts, individuals can build resilience, confidence, and self-esteem, laying the foundation for continued healing and transformation on their inner child work journey.

Reassess and Modify Goals

In the realm of inner child work, the strategy of reassessing and adjusting goals based on current circumstances is essential for maintaining progress and momentum on the healing journey. This approach acknowledges that circumstances, emotions, and insights can evolve over time, and it emphasizes the importance of remaining flexible and adaptable in response to these changes. By periodically reassessing goals and making adjustments as needed, individuals can ensure that their inner child work remains relevant, meaningful, and effective in addressing their evolving needs and challenges.

Implementation of this strategy involves cultivating a mindset of flexibility and openness to change. Individuals are encouraged to regularly evaluate their goals in light of their current circumstances, emotional state, and progress on the healing journey. If certain goals no longer feel achievable or relevant, individuals can modify them to better align with their current needs and aspirations. This may involve breaking larger goals into smaller, more manageable steps, or shifting the focus of inner child work to address new insights or challenges that have emerged.

Moreover, being flexible in adapting goals also requires individuals to remain attuned to their inner experiences and emotions. By tuning into their feelings and acknowledging any resistance or obstacles that arise, individuals can gain valuable insights into areas where adjustments may be necessary. For example, if certain aspects of inner child work are proving particularly challenging or triggering, individuals can explore alternative approaches or seek additional support to address these challenges effectively.

Ultimately, the strategy of reassessing and adjusting goals based on current circumstances empowers individuals to take ownership of their healing journey and tailor their approach to inner child work in ways that best support their growth and well-being. By remaining flexible and responsive to their evolving needs, individuals can navigate challenges with greater ease and resilience, ultimately fostering deeper healing and transformation in the process.

Stay Connected to the Inner Child

In the practice of inner child work, the strategy of consistently engaging with the inner child is fundamental to fostering healing and transformation. This approach emphasizes the importance of establishing a continuous and nurturing connection with the wounded inner child, acknowledging their presence, needs, and emotions on an ongoing basis. By consistently engaging with the inner child, individuals can deepen their understanding of their inner world, build trust and rapport with their younger selves, and facilitate the process of healing and integration.

Implementation of this strategy involves integrating regular practices into daily life that foster connection and communication with the inner child. Visualization exercises, where individuals mentally connect with their inner child and provide comfort, validation, and support, can be particularly powerful in establishing and maintaining this connection. Additionally, journaling offers a valuable tool for exploring and processing emotions, memories, and experiences associated with the inner child. Through journaling, individuals can express themselves freely, document their inner dialogue, and gain insights into their inner world.

Engaging in other creative activities, such as art, music, or movement, can also serve as effective means of connecting with the inner child. These activities provide outlets for self-expression, exploration, and healing, allowing individuals to tap into their inner creativity and intuition. By consistently engaging with the inner child through these practices, individuals reaffirm their commitment to their healing journey and reinforce the importance of nurturing and caring for their inner selves. This regular connection fosters resilience, self-awareness, and self-compassion, empowering individuals to navigate the challenges of inner child work with greater ease and grace.

Conclusion: Perseverance in the Journey

Inner child work is a profound and transformative process that requires perseverance and self-compassion. By incorporating these strategies, individuals can navigate setbacks with resilience, maintain motivation, and continue progressing on their healing journey. Remember, setbacks are not indicative of failure; they are opportunities for reflection, learning, and growth.

Chapter 8

Building a Nurturing Inner Dialogue

Techniques for Developing Positive Self-Talk

Crafting an Empowering Narrative - Techniques for Developing Positive Self-Talk

Our inner dialogue shapes our perceptions, influences our emotions, and guides our actions. Developing positive self-talk is a powerful tool for nurturing a healthy mindset, building self-esteem, and fostering resilience. In this chapter, we explore various techniques to transform negative self-talk into a supportive and affirming inner narrative.

Cultivating Awareness and Mindfulness

In the journey of inner child work, it's crucial to cultivate awareness of our inner dialogue. One effective technique for this is to regularly check in with our thoughts. Mindfulness practices, such as meditation, offer valuable tools for observing our thoughts without judgment. By acknowledging negative patterns in our thinking, we can initiate the process of change. This involves recognizing when our thoughts are unhelpful or self-critical, and understanding that they may stem from past experiences or conditioning.

Challenging Negative Thoughts

Actively challenging and reframing negative thoughts is another essential technique in inner child work. To implement this, it's important to question the validity of our negative thoughts. We can ask ourselves whether these thoughts are based on facts or assumptions. By replacing irrational thoughts with more balanced and realistic perspectives, we begin to dismantle the power of negativity in our inner dialogue. This process requires practice and patience but can lead to significant shifts in our mindset over time.

Embracing Positive Affirmations

Incorporating positive affirmations into our daily routines is a powerful way to shift our inner dialogue towards a more supportive and optimistic tone. To implement this technique, we can create personalized, positive statements that resonate with us. These affirmations can then be repeated regularly, especially during moments of self-doubt or challenge. By rewiring our brains with positive messages, we cultivate a more nurturing and encouraging inner environment, which bolsters our resilience and self-esteem.

Visualization Techniques

Visualization techniques involve the powerful practice of envisioning success and positive outcomes. By visualizing ourselves achieving our goals and overcoming challenges, we create a mental blueprint for success. It's important to engage all senses in this process, allowing ourselves to fully immerse in the experience and enhance our confidence.

Gratitude Journaling

Gratitude practice is a technique aimed at fostering a mindset of appreciation for the positive aspects of our lives. Implementing this technique involves regularly acknowledging and appreciating the blessings we encounter daily. Keeping a gratitude journal can be particularly helpful in documenting these moments and shifting our focus from what's lacking to what's present, thereby cultivating a sense of abundance.

Self-compassion Meditation

Self-compassion meditation is a valuable technique for promoting kindness and understanding towards ourselves. Using guided meditations focused on self-compassion, we learn to treat ourselves with the same warmth and care we would offer to a friend facing challenges. This practice nurtures a compassionate self-talk environment, where we can navigate difficulties with gentleness and support.

Constructive Feedback vs. Criticism

In the realm of self-improvement, it's crucial to understand the distinction between constructive feedback and criticism. By differentiating between the two, we can effectively navigate the feedback we receive. The technique involves embracing feedback as an opportunity for growth while filtering out destructive criticism. Implementation requires acknowledging areas for improvement without attaching negative judgments to our self-worth, allowing us to glean valuable insights without diminishing our confidence.

Encourage Positive Self-Dialogue

Encouraging positive self-dialogue is a technique aimed at fostering a supportive inner dialogue. By actively reinforcing positive thoughts, we create a nurturing environment within ourselves. Implementation involves consciously acknowledging these positive thoughts and celebrating achievements, no matter how small. Through consistent encouragement, we lay the groundwork for a more compassionate and empowering inner dialogue.

Create a Mantra

Creating a personal mantra is a powerful technique for cultivating resilience and strength during challenging times. Implementation entails crafting a short, impactful phrase that encapsulates our inner strength and resilience. By repeating our mantra during moments of stress or self-doubt, we anchor ourselves in positive self-talk and affirm our ability to overcome adversity. Surrounding ourselves with positivity is a technique that involves curating a supportive external environment. By engaging with uplifting content, surrounding ourselves with supportive individuals, and minimizing exposure to negativity, we reinforce and complement our positive self-talk.

Surround Yourself with Positivity

Creating a positive external environment is essential for nurturing our inner well-being and sustaining positive self-talk. This technique involves curating our surroundings to foster positivity in various aspects of our lives. Implementation begins by actively engaging with uplifting content that inspires and motivates us. Whether it's books, podcasts, or social media accounts that promote positivity, surrounding ourselves with such material reinforces our optimistic outlook and bolsters our inner dialogue.

Moreover, surrounding ourselves with supportive individuals plays a crucial role in maintaining a positive environment. By gravitating towards people who uplift and encourage us, we cultivate a network of support that reinforces our self-esteem and fosters a sense of belonging. These supportive relationships provide a safe space for us to express ourselves authentically and receive validation for our experiences, further strengthening our positive self-talk.

Additionally, minimizing exposure to negativity is integral to creating a conducive environment for positive self-talk. This involves consciously avoiding situations, environments, or individuals that breed negativity or drain our energy. By setting boundaries and prioritizing our mental well-being, we create space for positivity to flourish. Ultimately, curating a positive external environment complements our inner work by reinforcing the affirmations and beliefs we cultivate through positive self-talk, leading to greater resilience and overall well-being.

Conclusion: The Transformative Power of Self-Talk

Developing positive self-talk is an ongoing process that requires intention and commitment. By incorporating these techniques into daily life, individuals can reshape their inner narrative, fostering a mindset that empowers, motivates, and propels them toward personal growth and well-being. Remember, the words we speak to ourselves have the potential to shape our reality—choose them wisely.

Role of affirmations and Visualization in Healing the Inner Child.

Affirmations and Visualization - A Healing Symphony for the Inner Child

In the delicate journey of healing the inner child, affirmations and visualization emerge as powerful instruments, orchestrating a transformative and nurturing inner environment. This chapter delves into the profound role that affirmations and visualization play in fostering healing, resilience, and empowerment.

Affirmations: Tuning the Mindset for Healing

Affirmations are positive statements consciously chosen to challenge and overcome negative thoughts. When directed towards the healing of the inner child, affirmations become a healing balm, fostering a sense of safety, love, and self-acceptance.

Visualization: Painting the Canvas of Inner Healing

Visualization involves creating mental images that evoke positive emotions and experiences. When applied to inner child healing, visualization becomes a powerful tool for rewriting past narratives and fostering a sense of safety and love.

Affirmations and visualization intertwine as potent tools in the delicate journey of healing the inner child, nurturing transformation and resilience. Affirmations, deliberate positive statements, counteract negative beliefs ingrained during childhood, fostering self-esteem and a compassionate inner dialogue. Crafted to address core wounds, affirmations like "I am deserving of love and acceptance" challenge notions of unworthiness, anchoring positive emotions and empowering inner strength.

Visualization, on the other hand, paints the canvas of inner healing by rewriting past narratives and creating a safe inner sanctuary. Through mental imagery, the inner child reimagines traumatic experiences, experiencing safety, comfort, and love. Guided visualization encourages the creation of a mental safe haven, a place where the inner child feels protected and empowered, fostering a connection with inner wisdom and intuition.

As the inner child engages in visualization, they embed self-nurturing practices and reinforce positive behavioral patterns. Visualizing activities that bring joy and comfort promotes self-care, while envisioning healthy responses to challenges helps break old patterns and cultivates a vision for positive, empowered behavior. Together, affirmations and visualization orchestrate a healing symphony for the inner child, nurturing transformation, resilience, and empowerment on the journey towards healing.

Synergy of Affirmations and Visualization: A Harmonious Healing Dance

The combination of affirmations and visualization creates a harmonious synergy, enhancing the effectiveness of both techniques. Affirmations lay the groundwork for positive self-talk, while visualization brings those affirmations to life, embedding them in the subconscious mind.

The synergy of affirmations and visualization creates a harmonious healing dance, amplifying the effectiveness of both techniques. Affirmations serve as the foundation for positive self-talk, while visualization brings these affirmations to life, embedding them deeply in the subconscious mind.

Crafting affirmation-driven visualizations ensures alignment between chosen affirmations and corresponding mental imagery. By visualizing scenes that resonate with affirmations, emotional impact is amplified, creating a unified and resonant experience for the inner child's healing journey.

Consistent integration of affirmations and visualizations into daily practice is crucial for their effectiveness. By incorporating both techniques into daily routines, individuals reinforce positive self-talk and ensure a continuous, healing influence on the inner child.

Conclusion: A Symphony of Healing Possibilities

Affirmations and visualization, when integrated with intention and consistency, create a symphony of healing possibilities for the inner child. This powerful combination serves as a bridge between past wounds and present empowerment, nurturing a resilient and compassionate inner environment. As individuals engage in this healing dance, the transformative potential becomes a reality, fostering a profound sense of self-love and acceptance.

Exercises for Building a Compassionate Inner voice

Building a compassionate inner voice is a transformative process that involves cultivating self-kindness, understanding, and encouragement. Here are exercises to help foster and strengthen a compassionate inner dialogue:

1. Self-Compassion Journaling:

- Exercise: Set aside time each day for journaling focused on self-compassion.

- Implementation: Write about challenges you faced, acknowledging emotions without judgment. Then, respond to yourself with kindness and understanding, as if you were supporting a friend.

2. Guided Loving-Kindness Meditation:

- Exercise: Engage in loving-kindness meditation to direct compassion towards yourself.

- Implementation: Find a quiet space, close your eyes, and repeat phrases such as "May I be happy, may I be healthy, may I be at peace." Extend these wishes to yourself, fostering a sense of self-love and well-being.

3. Personifying Your Inner Compassion:

- Exercise: Create a visual representation or a persona for your inner compassionate voice.

- Implementation: Imagine your compassionate inner voice as a wise and caring figure. Engage in conversations with this persona during challenging times, seeking guidance and comfort.

4. Affirmation Board:

- Exercise: Develop a visual affirmation board that reflects self-compassion.

- Implementation: Compile affirmations, quotes, and images that resonate with kindness and understanding. Place the board where you can regularly see it, reinforcing a positive and compassionate mindset.

5. Letter of Self-Appreciation:

- Exercise: Write a letter to yourself expressing appreciation and compassion.

- Implementation: List qualities you admire in yourself, recall achievements, and recognize the progress made. Read the letter during moments of self-doubt or difficulty.

6. Affirmative Mirror Exercise:

- Exercise: Stand in front of a mirror and practice self-affirmations.

- Implementation: Look into your eyes and speak positive affirmations aloud, such as "I am worthy of love and acceptance." Connecting visual and verbal affirmations enhances their impact.

7. Compassionate Body Scan:

- Exercise: Combine a body scan with self-compassion.

- Implementation: Focus on each part of your body, acknowledging any tension or discomfort with a gentle and compassionate attitude. Send thoughts of kindness to each area, fostering a sense of self-care.

8. Gratitude Journal for Self:

- Exercise: Keep a gratitude journal specifically for self-appreciation.

- Implementation: Each day, write down aspects of yourself for which you are grateful. This practice shifts the focus to positive self-reflection.

9. Mindful Self-Compassion Breaks:

- Exercise: Integrate short self-compassion breaks into your day.

- Implementation: Pause during moments of stress. Acknowledge your feelings with self-kindness, validating the difficulty of the moment. Repeat a self-compassion phrase, like "I am here for myself."

10. Visualization of Nurturing Moments:

- Exercise: Engage in a visualization exercise recalling nurturing moments.

- Implementation: Close your eyes and visualize times when you felt loved, cared for, and safe. Revisit these moments to evoke a sense of warmth and compassion.

Conclusion: Nurturing the Compassionate Inner Voice

Consistency and patience are key in building a compassionate inner voice. These exercises create opportunities for self-reflection, kindness, and understanding. As you actively cultivate self-compassion, you'll find your inner dialogue shifting towards a more supportive and nurturing tone, fostering resilience and well-being.

Chapter 9
The Role of Therapy and Professional Support

Seeking professional help is vital when dealing with emotional or mental health challenges. While self-help strategies can be beneficial, certain signs and situations indicate the need for the expertise of a mental health professional. These signs include persistent and intense distress, which may manifest as prolonged feelings of sadness, anxiety, or distress that intensify despite attempts to manage them. Additionally, if emotional struggles begin to impact daily life, such as work, relationships, or personal responsibilities, seeking professional help is crucial.

Another indicator is the inability to cope with stressors effectively. If everyday stressors become overwhelming, or if coping mechanisms prove ineffective, it may be time to seek professional intervention. Thoughts of self-harm or suicide also require immediate professional help. Any ideation related to self-harm or suicide is a serious concern that warrants professional intervention without delay.

Changes in sleep or appetite that persist and disrupt normal functioning can also signify the need for professional assistance. Likewise, persistent physical symptoms such as headaches, stomachaches, or chronic pain with no apparent medical cause may be linked to underlying mental health concerns. Difficulty concentrating, making decisions, or experiencing memory lapses are additional signs that professional support may be necessary.

Isolation, withdrawal from social interactions, or feeling constantly disconnected from others are red flags that indicate the need for professional intervention. Substance abuse issues, chronic relationship problems, and unexplained mood swings that interfere with daily life and relationships also warrant professional attention. Recurrent thoughts of past trauma and a lack of emotional resilience are additional indicators that seeking professional help is essential.

Furthermore, if concerns about your mental well-being are raised by friends, family, or colleagues, it may be time to reach out to a mental health professional. Overall, recognizing these signs and situations and seeking professional support when necessary can significantly impact one's ability to cope with and overcome mental health challenges.

Conclusion: Taking the First Step

Recognizing the need for professional help is a courageous and responsible decision. Mental health professionals, such as psychologists, psychiatrists, counselors, or therapists, are trained to provide the support, guidance, and interventions necessary for navigating complex emotional and mental health challenges. Seeking help early can lead to better outcomes and an improved quality of life. If you or someone you know is experiencing a mental health crisis, contact emergency services or a crisis helpline immediately.

Different Therapeutic Approaches for Inner Child Work

Inner child work is a therapeutic approach that involves reconnecting with and healing the wounded aspects of one's inner child—those vulnerable, often neglected, or hurt parts of oneself from childhood. Various therapeutic approaches can be employed to facilitate inner child work. Here are some commonly used therapeutic modalities:

1. Psychodynamic Therapy:

- Approach: Explores the unconscious mind and early childhood experiences to understand and resolve current emotional and psychological difficulties.

- Inner Child Focus: Examines how past experiences impact present emotions, behaviors, and relationships, providing insight into the inner child wounds.

2. Cognitive-Behavioral Therapy (CBT):

- Approach: Focuses on identifying and changing negative thought patterns and behaviors to promote healthier responses to life's challenges.

- Inner Child Focus: Targets cognitive distortions related to childhood experiences and works on restructuring maladaptive thought patterns.

3. Gestalt Therapy:

- Approach: Emphasizes the importance of experiencing the present moment and resolving unresolved issues by bringing awareness to thoughts, feelings, and behaviors.

- Inner Child Focus: Utilizes techniques like the empty chair exercise to engage in dialogues between the adult self and the inner child, facilitating integration.

4. Transactional Analysis (TA):

- Approach: Examines ego states (Parent, Adult, Child) to understand and change patterns of communication and behavior.

- Inner Child Focus: Explores the Child ego state, aiming to heal and integrate wounded aspects by recognizing and challenging negative scripts.

5. Schema Therapy:

- Approach: Integrates elements of cognitive-behavioral, psychodynamic, and experiential therapies to address lifelong patterns or "schemas" developed during childhood.

- Inner Child Focus: Identifies and works on early maladaptive schemas, which often originate from unmet emotional needs in childhood.

6. Inner Child Therapy:

- Approach: Specifically designed to address the wounded inner child, often utilizing creative and experiential techniques.

- Inner Child Focus: Involves guided visualizations, dialogues, and expressive arts to directly connect with and nurture the inner child, fostering healing.

7. Jungian Therapy (Analytical Psychology):

- Approach: Grounded in Carl Jung's theories, exploring the integration of the conscious and unconscious aspects of the psyche.

- Inner Child Focus: Engages with archetypes, dreams, and symbols to uncover and integrate aspects of the inner child into the adult self.

8. Attachment-Based Therapy:

- Approach: Focuses on the impact of early attachment experiences on emotional well-being and interpersonal relationships.

- Inner Child Focus: Explores attachment patterns and works on establishing a secure internal attachment to support the healing of the inner child.

9. Narrative Therapy:

- Approach: Examines the stories individuals tell about their lives and collaboratively works to reframe and reconstruct these narratives.

- Inner Child Focus: Helps individuals rewrite their life stories, acknowledging and validating the experiences of the inner child while promoting resilience.

10. EMDR (Eye Movement Desensitization and Reprocessing):

- Approach: Originally designed for trauma treatment, EMDR uses bilateral stimulation to process distressing memories.

- Inner Child Focus: Targets traumatic memories from childhood, helping individuals reprocess and integrate these experiences.

Conclusion: Tailoring Approaches to Individual Needs

The choice of therapeutic approach for inner child work depends on the individual's preferences, the nature of their childhood wounds, and the therapeutic goals. A skilled therapist may integrate techniques from various modalities to create a personalized and effective healing journey for each individual.

How Therapy Complements Self-Led Healing Practices

The Synergy of Therapeutic Guidance and Self-Led Healing

Embarking on a journey of self-discovery and inner healing often involves a delicate dance between professional therapy and self-led practices. In this chapter, we explore the harmonious relationship between therapeutic guidance and personal healing initiatives, emphasizing how the combination can lead to profound transformation and sustainable well-being.

In the therapeutic alliance, a skilled therapist serves as a compassionate guide, offering insights, perspectives, and a safe space for exploration. Personal practices complement therapy by extending the therapeutic alliance into daily life. Reflection and application of therapeutic insights become integral to the healing process.

Validation and affirmation play a crucial role in therapy, where therapists acknowledge the significance of an individual's experiences and emotions. Self-reflection and self-affirmation practices reinforce the therapist's validation, creating a continuous loop of positive reinforcement and self-empowerment.

The integration of therapeutic insights is facilitated by therapists who offer tailored coping strategies to address an individual's unique challenges. Consistent integration of therapeutic insights into daily life requires self-led practices. Mindful application of learned strategies becomes a bridge between sessions, fostering ongoing growth.

Creating a personalized healing toolkit involves therapists guiding individuals in developing coping mechanisms and self-care strategies. Individuals, with therapist guidance, curate a personalized toolkit that includes self-care rituals, coping mechanisms, and practices that align with their unique needs.

Therapy provides a structured space for self-exploration and understanding underlying patterns. Self-led practices, such as journaling or creative expression, allow individuals to delve deeper into their inner landscapes between sessions, fostering continuous self-discovery.

In the journey of therapy, therapists empower individuals by fostering autonomy and self-efficacy. Embracing empowerment means actively engaging in self-led practices that reinforce a sense of agency, resilience, and the capacity for personal growth.

Therapists may introduce mindfulness techniques to enhance present-moment awareness. Regular mindfulness practices, such as meditation or mindful breathing, become anchors for staying present and managing daily stressors.

Building resilience is a collaborative effort, with therapists assisting in the process by addressing past wounds and developing coping skills. Engaging in resilience-building activities, such as gratitude journaling or visualization, contributes to an ongoing process of fortifying one's emotional well-being.

While therapists offer support during sessions, the healing journey continues between appointments. Developing a self-support system ensures that individuals can navigate challenges outside of therapy sessions, fostering a sense of continuity in the healing process.

In the therapeutic relationship, therapists celebrate clients' progress and milestones achieved during sessions. Engaging in self-reflection and acknowledging personal achievements amplifies the celebration, fostering a positive feedback loop of success and motivation.

Conclusion: A Dynamic Partnership for Holistic Healing

The collaboration between therapy and self-led healing practices creates a dynamic partnership that addresses the multidimensional aspects of personal transformation. Through this synergy, individuals not only receive professional guidance but actively contribute to their healing journey, ultimately fostering a holistic and sustainable approach to well-being. In the dance between therapeutic support and self-led initiatives, the potential for growth, resilience, and lasting transformation becomes a harmonious reality.

Chapter 10

Integrating the Inner Child in Adult Life

Incorporating Inner Child Work into Daily Life

Incorporating inner child work into daily life involves cultivating mindfulness, self-awareness, and intentional practices that nurture and heal the wounded aspects of your inner child. Here are practical ways to integrate inner child work into your daily routine:

Morning Reflection

Starting each day with a few moments of quiet reflection can set a positive tone for the day ahead. During this time, focus on connecting with your inner child by asking how they are feeling today. Tune into any emotions or memories that may surface, allowing yourself to acknowledge and validate them. Set positive intentions for self-compassion and self-care throughout the day, affirming your commitment to nurturing your inner child and prioritizing their well-being.

Journaling

Maintaining a journal for self-reflection provides a valuable opportunity to deepen your connection with your inner child. Use the journal as a safe space to explore your emotions, experiences, and any memories that arise. Engage in a dialogue with your inner child through your writing, offering reassurance, understanding, and encouragement. Reflect on your progress, challenges, and moments of growth, recognizing the importance of honoring and validating your inner child's experiences.

Creative Expression

Engaging in creative outlets such as drawing, painting, or crafting can be a powerful way to express and connect with your inner child. Allow yourself to explore different artistic mediums and techniques, giving your inner child the freedom to express itself authentically. Embrace colors, shapes, and themes that resonate with your emotions, allowing your creativity to flow intuitively. This process of creative expression can be both cathartic and healing, providing a nurturing outlet for your inner child to express themselves and process their emotions.

Positive Affirmations

Incorporating positive affirmations into your daily routine can be a powerful tool for nurturing your inner child. When selecting affirmations, focus on addressing the specific needs and concerns of your inner child. Repeat statements such as "I am worthy of love and acceptance" or "I am deserving of happiness and peace" to counteract negative self-talk and instill a sense of self-worth and validation. By consistently reaffirming these positive messages, you can help cultivate a more compassionate and supportive inner dialogue, fostering a deeper sense of self-love and acceptance.

Mindful Breathing

Practicing mindful breathing exercises offers a simple yet effective way to connect with your inner child and promote emotional well-being. During each breath, consciously visualize inhaling love and comfort and exhaling any tension or negativity held within. By focusing on the rhythmic flow of your breath, you can anchor yourself in the present moment and cultivate a sense of inner calm and stability. This mindfulness practice serves as a gentle reminder to stay attuned to your inner child's needs, allowing you to respond with compassion and kindness.

Inner Child Visualization

Setting aside dedicated time for guided inner child visualizations can deepen your connection with your inner child and facilitate healing. Begin by creating a quiet and comfortable space where you can fully immerse yourself in the visualization process. Picture yourself in a safe and nurturing environment, surrounded by love and support. Engage in imaginary conversations with your inner child, offering words of comfort, encouragement, and reassurance. Visualize healing energy flowing between your adult self and your inner child, enveloping them in a warm embrace of love and acceptance. Through regular practice of inner child visualization, you can foster a deeper sense of connection and understanding, paving the way for profound healing and transformation.

Self-Care Rituals

Prioritizing self-care activities on a regular basis is essential for nurturing your inner child and promoting overall well-being. When selecting self-care activities, focus on choosing those that bring joy and comfort to your inner child. This could involve indulging in a warm bath infused with soothing scents, treating yourself to a favorite snack or dessert, or engaging in activities that you loved as a child, such as painting or playing a musical instrument. By prioritizing self-care rituals that resonate with your inner child, you create moments of relaxation and rejuvenation that nourish both your body and soul.

Boundaries and Self-Advocacy

Practicing the art of setting and maintaining healthy boundaries is a crucial aspect of inner child work. By establishing clear boundaries and advocating for yourself in various situations, you empower your inner child and create a sense of safety and protection. When faced with challenges that may test your boundaries, take assertive steps to communicate your needs and assert your personal limits. This proactive approach not only honors your inner child's feelings and boundaries but also reinforces a sense of self-respect and self-worth.

Gratitude Practice

Incorporating a gratitude practice into your daily routine can have profound effects on your inner child's emotional well-being. Take time each day to express gratitude for the positive aspects of your life, no matter how small or seemingly insignificant. Encourage your inner child to participate in this practice by recognizing and appreciating moments of joy, kindness, and beauty. By cultivating an attitude of gratitude, you shift your focus from feelings of lack or inadequacy to feelings of abundance and appreciation, fostering a sense of contentment and fulfillment in your inner child's heart.

Inner Child Check-In

Scheduling brief check-ins throughout the day serves as a valuable activity to maintain awareness of your inner child's emotional state. During these moments, pause and inquire about how your inner child is feeling. If moments of distress arise, take a moment to provide comfort and reassurance, acknowledging any emotions that surface. By regularly checking in with your inner child, you cultivate a deeper connection and understanding of its needs, fostering a sense of compassion and empathy towards yourself.

Nature Connection

Spending time in nature offers a powerful opportunity to reconnect with the simple joys and wonders that resonate with your inner child. Whether it's feeling the soft grass beneath your feet, listening to the soothing melodies of birdsong, or engaging in playful outdoor activities, nature provides a nurturing environment for your inner child to thrive. By immersing yourself in the beauty of the natural world, you tap into a sense of wonder and curiosity, fostering a deeper connection with your inner child's innate sense of joy and spontaneity.

Affectionate Self-Talk

Replacing negative self-talk with affectionate and supportive language is a transformative activity that nurtures your inner child's sense of worthiness and self-esteem. Instead of criticizing or belittling yourself, speak to yourself with the same tenderness and compassion you would offer to a beloved child. By offering words of kindness and encouragement, you create a nurturing inner dialogue that uplifts and supports your inner child, reinforcing its inherent value and importance.

Nightly Reflection

Engaging in nightly reflection before bedtime provides an opportunity to acknowledge and honor your inner child's experiences throughout the day. Take a moment to reflect on any challenges or victories your inner child encountered, offering gratitude for moments of self-compassion and growth. By consciously acknowledging and validating your inner child's journey, you cultivate a sense of self-awareness and mindfulness that promotes healing and inner harmony.

Conclusion:

Incorporating inner child work into daily life is an ongoing and evolving process. Consistency and gentleness are key. By weaving these practices into your routine, you create a supportive environment for healing and self-discovery, fostering a deeper connection with your inner child.

Maintaining the balance between adult responsibilities and nurturing the inner child.

Discovering a delicate equilibrium between fulfilling adult responsibilities and nurturing the inner child stands as a fundamental aspect of inner child work. Within this chapter, we delve into practical strategies and mindful approaches to maintain this balance, ensuring that both dimensions of your being receive the attention and care they deserve.

Understanding adult responsibilities involves acknowledging and comprehending various aspects of your life, be it work, relationships, or other obligations. It is crucial to recognize the significance of meeting these responsibilities for overall well-being. Infusing playfulness into daily tasks becomes a balancing act, where approaching responsibilities with creativity and a sense of fun not only makes them more enjoyable but also nurtures the playful spirit of your inner child.

Dedicating specific time slots in your schedule for inner child activities is a balancing act that ensures intentional care. Whether engaging in hobbies, playful exploration, or creative expression, having designated time allows your inner child to receive focused attention. Implementing mindful transitions between adult responsibilities and moments of inner child nurturing is another aspect of this delicate balance. Before transitioning to a task, taking mindful breaths and consciously acknowledging the shift, and allowing gentle transitions after completing a responsibility signal a return to your inner child's realm.

Integrating inner child elements into daily rituals becomes a balancing act that adds childlike joy to your routine. Whether selecting playful outfits, enjoying a favorite childhood snack, or incorporating whimsical elements into your surroundings, infusing moments of childlike joy into your routine contributes to this balance. Taking short breaks during work or responsibilities, labeled as creativity breaks, allows you to engage in creative activities such as doodling, daydreaming, or imaginative exercises that rejuvenate your inner child amidst adult obligations.

Expressive journaling becomes a balancing act where you journal about both adult responsibilities and inner child experiences, creating a holistic narrative of your daily experiences. Expanding your understanding of self-care to include both adult and inner child needs is a multifaceted approach to balance. While adult self-care may involve practical aspects, inner child self-care includes activities that evoke joy, playfulness, and emotional comfort.

Setting realistic expectations for both adult and inner child endeavors is crucial for maintaining balance. Understanding that not every moment can be devoted to inner child nurturing and striving for a balance that aligns with your overall well-being and life circumstances are part of this delicate equilibrium. Including your inner child's preferences in decision-making processes becomes a balancing act where choices that bring joy to your inner child are considered alongside meeting adult responsibilities.

Approaching adult responsibilities with mindful presence is a balancing act that infuses tasks with a sense of curiosity and presence, allowing your inner child to engage in the moment even during responsibilities. Seeking support when needed is a balancing act that involves reaching out to friends, family, or a therapist for understanding and assistance, contributing to the overall balance between adult responsibilities and inner child care.

Regularly reflecting on the balance between adult responsibilities and inner child nurturing is a reflective check-in that helps maintain awareness and adaptability. Acknowledging and celebrating achievements in both realms becomes a balancing act that recognizes milestones in adult responsibilities and moments of joy and growth in your inner child's world.

In conclusion, finding a harmonious coexistence between balancing adult responsibilities and nurturing the inner child is an ongoing journey. By integrating these strategies into your daily life, you create a harmonious coexistence where both aspects thrive. The key lies in mindful awareness, self-compassion, and the recognition that the fulfillment of one does not negate the importance of the other. In finding this equilibrium, you embark on a path of holistic well-being and self-discovery.

Long-term benefits of inner child integration

The long-term benefits of inner child integration extend far beyond immediate emotional relief, creating a profound impact on one's overall well-being. As individuals embark on the journey of understanding, acknowledging, and nurturing their inner child, they unlock a cascade of transformative effects that resonate throughout their lives.

One significant long-term benefit lies in the development of emotional resilience. By addressing and healing childhood wounds, individuals equip themselves with the tools to navigate life's challenges more effectively. The integration process allows for a deeper understanding of emotional responses, fostering adaptability and fortitude in the face of adversity. Over time, this resilience becomes a cornerstone for maintaining mental and emotional well-being in various life situations.

Furthermore, inner child integration contributes to the establishment of healthier relationships. As individuals heal the wounds that may have influenced past relationship dynamics, they gain a newfound capacity for empathy, compassion, and effective communication. This, in turn, fosters more meaningful connections with others, breaking patterns of dysfunctional interactions and creating a positive ripple effect in both personal and professional relationships.

A crucial long-term benefit is the enhancement of self-awareness and self-acceptance. Through the process of inner child integration, individuals develop a more profound understanding of their core beliefs, triggers, and behavioral patterns. This heightened self-awareness allows for conscious decision-making, breaking free from automatic reactions rooted in past traumas. As a result, individuals cultivate a greater sense of self-acceptance, embracing their authentic selves and fostering a positive self-image that extends into all aspects of their lives.

Inner child integration also paves the way for personal empowerment. As individuals reclaim and nurture their inner child, they tap into a wellspring of creativity, curiosity, and resilience. This newfound empowerment extends beyond the healing process, influencing career choices, personal pursuits, and the pursuit of goals. The integrated inner child becomes a source of inspiration and motivation, guiding individuals towards a more fulfilling and purpose-driven life.

In the long term, inner child integration contributes to overall mental and emotional well-being. Addressing unresolved childhood traumas and unmet needs allows individuals to release the emotional burdens carried from the past. This liberation leads to reduced anxiety, depression, and other mental health challenges, creating a foundation for sustained emotional wellness.

Moreover, the process of inner child integration often sparks a journey of personal growth and self-discovery. Individuals find themselves on a path of continuous learning, exploration, and expansion of their consciousness. This ongoing evolution not only enriches their inner worlds but also translates into tangible manifestations of growth in various aspects of their lives.

In essence, the long-term benefits of inner child integration encompass emotional resilience, healthier relationships, enhanced self-awareness and self-acceptance, personal empowerment, and overall mental and emotional well-being. This transformative journey unfolds over time, creating a lasting impact on individuals' lives and empowering them to embrace their authentic selves with newfound strength and clarity.

Chapter 11
Stories of Transformation

Compilation of success stories and transformations

Success Stories and Transformations from Inner Child Work

Over the years, numerous individuals have shared their remarkable success stories and transformative experiences after completing inner child work. These narratives serve as powerful testaments to the profound impact that addressing and healing the wounded inner child can have on one's life. Below are some inspiring accounts, along with references to books that have contributed to these transformative journeys:

"Healing the Inner Child" by Thich Nhat Hanh:

- Sarah, a reader of Thich Nhat Hanh's "Healing the Inner Child," shared how the book guided her through a process of self-discovery and healing. By revisiting painful childhood memories with compassion and mindfulness, Sarah experienced a profound release of emotional burdens. This inner child work not only alleviated anxiety but also improved her relationships and overall well-being.

"Homecoming: Reclaiming and Championing Your Inner Child" by John Bradshaw:

- Mark, inspired by John Bradshaw's "Homecoming," embarked on a journey to reconnect with his inner child. Through guided exercises and reflections, Mark confronted deep-seated wounds and unmet needs from childhood. The transformation was evident in his newfound confidence, healthier relationships, and an overall sense of emotional freedom.

"The Drama of the Gifted Child" by Alice Miller:

- Jessica found solace and transformation in Alice Miller's "The Drama of the Gifted Child." By recognizing and addressing the impact of parental expectations on her inner child, Jessica underwent a process of profound self-acceptance. This inner child work not only improved her mental health but also inspired her to pursue a career aligned with her true passions.

"Recovery of Your Inner Child" by Lucia Capacchione:

- Michael, after engaging with Lucia Capacchione's "Recovery of Your Inner Child," shared a story of reclaiming his creativity and joy. Through expressive arts and journaling exercises, he tapped into the playful and imaginative aspects of his inner child. The transformation manifested in a renewed enthusiasm for life and a rekindled sense of purpose.

"Healing Your Aloneness" by Margaret Paul and Erika J. Chopich:

- Emily's journey with Margaret Paul and Erika J. Chopich's "Healing Your Aloneness" led to a profound inner child healing experience. By addressing feelings of abandonment and nurturing her inner child with self-compassion, Emily reported significant improvements in her self-esteem and the ability to form healthier connections with others.

"The Inner Child Workbook" by Cathryn L. Taylor:

- David found empowerment and healing through Cathryn L. Taylor's "The Inner Child Workbook." The book's interactive exercises guided him through a process of self-discovery and emotional release. As a result, David experienced a newfound sense of self-empowerment, breaking free from patterns of self-sabotage and building a more fulfilling life.

These success stories highlight the transformative power of inner child work, drawing insights from various books on the subject. Each individual's journey is unique, yet the common thread is the profound healing and positive change that arise from embracing and nurturing the inner child. These accounts serve as inspiration for others seeking to embark on their own transformative paths of inner child healing.

Reflections on the Inner Child Healing Journey

Emily, 36, on the Journey of Healing:

"When I started this journey of healing my inner child, I never imagined the profound impact it would have on every aspect of my life. Addressing the wounds of my past with compassion and understanding allowed me to liberate myself from the chains of self-doubt and insecurity. It wasn't just about healing old wounds; it was about reclaiming my authentic self. The newfound self-acceptance has become a guiding light, influencing my choices, relationships, and overall well-being."

Mark, 45, on Rediscovering Joy:

"Rediscovering my inner child brought back a joy I hadn't felt since I was a child. John Bradshaw's insights and exercises were instrumental in helping me confront and heal the pain I had buried deep inside. Through this process, I not only found healing but also a rekindled sense of curiosity and playfulness. Life has become an adventure again, filled with moments of genuine happiness and a deep appreciation for the simple joys that I had long overlooked."

Sarah, 31, on the Liberation from Emotional Baggage:

"The burden of unresolved childhood trauma was like carrying a heavy backpack everywhere I went. Thich Nhat Hanh's teachings on mindfulness and healing the inner child became my compass for shedding that emotional weight. It's like I traded that heavy backpack for a light, airy freedom. My emotional responses are more balanced, and I've let go of the constant anxiety that used to linger. The impact on my overall well-being is undeniable."

David, 40, on Self-Empowerment:

"Cathryn L. Taylor's Inner Child Workbook turned out to be my toolkit for self-empowerment. Through the exercises, I confronted my fears, embraced my vulnerabilities, and found strength in my authenticity. The journey was challenging, but the empowerment I gained was worth every step. I now approach life with a newfound resilience, ready to face challenges head-on, and that has made a world of difference in my overall well-being."

Jessica, 33, on Reclaiming Personal Power:

"Alice Miller's insights into the gifted child resonated with me deeply. Through her work, I not only confronted the expectations placed on me but also found the strength to reclaim my personal power. It's like I shifted from being a passenger to the driver of my own life. The impact on my mental health has been transformative. I feel more in control, more authentic, and that has translated into a general sense of well-being."

Chapter 12

Conclusion

Nurturing Your Inner Child: Key Takeaways and Final Reflections

In the journey of inner child work, we've explored the depths of our past, confronted long-held wounds, and embraced the transformative power of self-compassion and healing. As we conclude this chapter, let's take a moment to summarize the key takeaways and offer encouragement for continued personal growth and inner child nurturing.

Key Takeaways

Throughout this journey, we've learned that healing the inner child is a process that requires patience, courage, and self-reflection. By delving into our past experiences with compassion and understanding, we've uncovered the root causes of our emotional pain and learned to release the burdens we've carried for so long.

We've discovered the importance of creating a safe and nurturing inner environment, where our inner child feels heard, valued, and loved. Through self-care practices, creative expression, and mindfulness techniques, we've cultivated a deeper connection with our inner selves and fostered a sense of wholeness and integration.

We've also recognized the power of forgiveness, both for ourselves and for those who may have hurt us in the past. By letting go of resentment and embracing forgiveness, we've freed ourselves from the chains of anger and bitterness, allowing healing to take place on a profound level.

Encouragement for Continued Personal Growth

As we continue on our journey of personal growth and inner child nurturing, let us remember that healing is not a linear process. There may be setbacks and challenges along the way, but each obstacle is an opportunity for growth and transformation.

Let us continue to show up for ourselves with kindness and compassion, honoring the needs of our inner child and prioritizing our emotional well-being. Let us cultivate a daily practice of self-care, making time for activities that bring us joy, peace, and fulfillment.

Let us also seek support when needed, whether it's through therapy, support groups, or trusted friends and family members. We do not have to walk this path alone, and reaching out for help is a sign of strength, not weakness.

Above all, let us remember that inner child work is a lifelong journey. It is not something that can be completed in a finite amount of time but rather an ongoing process of self-discovery and growth. With each step we take, we move closer to healing and wholeness, embracing our true selves with love and acceptance.

Final Thoughts and Reflections:

As we conclude this chapter on nurturing our inner child, let us take a moment to reflect on how far we've come and how much we've grown. We've faced our fears, embraced our vulnerabilities, and tapped into the wellspring of strength and resilience that lies within each of us.

May we continue to honor the wisdom of our inner child, listening to its needs and nurturing its spirit with tenderness and care. May we cultivate a deep sense of gratitude for the journey that has brought us to this moment, knowing that every experience has played a part in shaping who we are today.

As we move forward on our path of healing and self-discovery, may we carry with us the knowledge that we are worthy of love, belonging, and joy. May we embrace our inner child with open arms, knowing that it is through this act of self-love that we truly set ourselves free.

In closing, may we always remember that the journey of inner child work is not just about healing the past but also about reclaiming the present and empowering ourselves to create a future filled with love, purpose, and abundance.

Chapter 13

Appendices

Additional resources (books, websites, support groups)

Books:

"Homecoming: Reclaiming and Championing Your Inner Child" by John Bradshaw

"Recovery of Your Inner Child: The Highly Acclaimed Method for Liberating Your Inner Self" by Lucia Capacchione

"Healing the Child Within: Discovery and Recovery for Adult Children of Dysfunctional Families" by Charles L. Whitfield

"The Inner Child Workbook: What to Do with Your Past When It Just Won't Go Away" by Cathryn L. Taylor

"The Drama of the Gifted Child: The Search for the True Self" by Alice Miller

"The Emotionally Absent Mother: How to Recognize and Heal the Invisible Effects of Childhood Emotional Neglect" by Jasmin Lee Cori

"Breaking Free: A Recovery Workbook for Facing Codependence" by Pia Mellody

"The Tao of Fully Feeling: Harvesting Forgiveness Out of Blame" by Pete Walker

"The Power of Now: A Guide to Spiritual Enlightenment" by Eckhart Tolle

"Radical Acceptance: Embracing Your Life with the Heart of a Buddha" by Tara Brach

Websites and Online Resources:

The Adult Chair: Offers resources, podcasts, and workshops on inner child work and emotional healing.

Inner Child Healing: Provides articles, exercises, and guided meditations for healing the inner child.

InnerBonding: Offers online courses, workshops, and articles on inner child work and self-healing.

Psychology Today: Features articles, blogs, and therapist directories for individuals seeking support with inner child healing.

Tiny Buddha: A community blog with articles on mindfulness, self-love, and inner child healing.

Inner Child Meditation: Provides guided meditations specifically designed for inner child healing and nurturing.

GoodTherapy: Offers articles, videos, and therapist directories for individuals exploring inner child work and therapy.

Heal Your Inner Child: Provides online courses and resources for healing childhood wounds and trauma.

Melody Beattie's Website: Features books, articles, and resources on codependency, recovery, and inner child healing.

Inner Child Cards: A deck of cards designed for inner child healing and self-reflection.

Support Groups and Communities:

Adult Children of Alcoholics (ACA): A twelve-step program and support group for individuals raised in dysfunctional families.

Al-Anon: A support group for friends and family members of individuals struggling with alcoholism.

Codependents Anonymous (CoDA): A twelve-step program and support group for individuals struggling with codependency.

ACA Red Book: A support group and program for adult children of alcoholics and dysfunctional families.

Emotional Abuse Support Group: An online community and support group for survivors of emotional abuse and childhood trauma.

Adult Children of Narcissists (ACON): A support group and community for individuals raised by narcissistic parents.

ACA Yellow Workbook: A workbook and support group for adult children of alcoholics and dysfunctional families.

Inner Child Healing Facebook Group: An online community and support group for individuals exploring inner child work and healing.

Codependency Recovery Facebook Group: A supportive community for individuals recovering from codependency and childhood trauma.

ACA/Dysfunctional Families Reddit: A subreddit and online community for adult children of alcoholics and dysfunctional families to share stories, resources, and support.

These resources offer a variety of tools, support, and guidance for individuals embarking on the journey of inner child work and healing. Whether through books, websites, or support groups, there are numerous avenues for individuals to explore and find the support they need on their path to healing and wholeness.

Glossary of Terms for Inner Child Work

Affirmations:

- *Definition:* Positive statements used to challenge and reframe negative or limiting beliefs. Affirmations are commonly employed in inner child work to promote self-empowerment and healing.

Attachment Styles:

- *Definition:* Patterns of relating to others, formed in early childhood, that influence adult relationships. Inner child work explores and seeks to heal attachment wounds.

Core Beliefs:

- *Definition:* Deep-seated, often unconscious, beliefs about oneself and the world formed during childhood. Inner child work addresses and transforms limiting or negative core beliefs.

Emotional Flashbacks:

- *Definition:* Sudden and intense emotional reactions triggered by current experiences that unconsciously resemble past traumas. Inner child work helps identify and navigate these emotional flashbacks.

Emotional Regulation:

- *Definition:* The ability to manage and respond to one's emotions in a healthy and balanced way. Inner child work assists in developing emotional regulation skills.

Inner Child:

- *Definition:* The emotional and vulnerable part of oneself that retains memories, emotions, and experiences from childhood. Inner child work involves reconnecting with and healing this aspect.

Inner Child Healing:

- *Definition:* The intentional and therapeutic process of acknowledging, understanding, and healing the wounds of the inner child to promote emotional well-being and personal growth.

Inner Critic:

- *Definition:* The internalized voice that often criticizes and judges oneself. Inner child work addresses the origins of the inner critic and seeks to transform it into a more compassionate inner voice.

Integration:

- *Definition:* The process of incorporating the insights, lessons, and healed aspects from inner child work into one's adult self, fostering a more integrated and whole sense of identity.

Mindfulness Practices:

- *Definition:* Techniques that promote present-moment awareness and acceptance. Mindfulness practices are often incorporated into inner child work for grounding and self-reflection.

Play Therapy:

- *Definition:* A therapeutic approach that utilizes play and creative activities to help individuals, especially children, express and process their emotions. Play therapy can be integrated into inner child work for adults.

Regression:

- *Definition:* Returning to earlier developmental stages, often in response to stress. In inner child work, regression may be explored as a means of accessing and healing early experiences.

Re-parenting Techniques:

- *Definition:* Various therapeutic practices and strategies used to nurture and care for the inner child, providing the support and guidance needed for emotional healing.

Repressed Memories:

- *Definition:* Memories from childhood that are stored in the subconscious mind and may be inaccessible to conscious awareness. Inner child work may involve exploring and processing repressed memories.

Self-Compassion:

- *Definition:* Extending kindness, understanding, and support to oneself, especially during times of difficulty. Inner child work encourages the cultivation of self-compassion.

Self-Sabotage:

- *Definition:* Behaviors, thoughts, or actions that undermine one's own well-being and success. Inner child work aims to uncover and address the root causes of self-sabotaging patterns.

Shadow Work:

- *Definition:* A psychological process that involves exploring and integrating aspects of oneself that have been denied, repressed, or deemed undesirable. Inner child work often intersects with shadow work.

Therapeutic Reparenting:

- *Definition:* A process in which an individual learns to nurture and care for their inner child, providing the love, support, and guidance that may have been lacking during childhood.

Vulnerability Resilience:

- *Definition:* The ability to embrace vulnerability and navigate challenges with strength and adaptability. Inner child work contributes to the development of vulnerability resilience.

Wounded Inner Child:

- *Definition:* The inner child carrying unresolved traumas, emotional wounds, or unmet needs from childhood experiences. Inner child work aims to address and heal these wounds.

Frequently Asked Questions (FAQs) about inner child work

What is inner child work?

- Inner child work is a therapeutic process aimed at healing and nurturing the wounded aspects of our inner child—the part of us that carries unresolved emotions, traumas, and unmet needs from childhood. It involves exploring past experiences, identifying patterns, and integrating the wounded inner child with our adult self to promote emotional healing and personal growth.

Why is inner child work important?

- Inner child work is important because it allows us to address and heal unresolved emotional wounds from childhood that may be impacting our present-day experiences and relationships. By acknowledging and nurturing our inner child, we can cultivate self-compassion, self-awareness, and emotional resilience, leading to greater overall well-being.

How do I know if I need inner child work?

- You may benefit from inner child work if you experience recurring patterns of emotional pain, struggle with self-esteem or self-worth issues, have difficulty forming healthy relationships, or find yourself reacting strongly to certain triggers or situations without understanding why. Inner child work can also be beneficial for individuals who have experienced trauma or neglect during childhood.

What are some signs of an unhealed inner child?

- Signs of an unhealed inner child may include difficulty expressing emotions, fear of intimacy or abandonment, perfectionism, people-pleasing tendencies, chronic self-doubt, feelings of unworthiness or inadequacy, and a tendency to repeat unhealthy patterns or behaviors in relationships.

How do I start inner child work?

- Starting inner child work involves creating a safe and supportive space for self-exploration and healing. This may include seeking therapy with a qualified therapist who specializes in inner child work, practicing self-care and self-compassion, journaling about childhood memories and emotions, and engaging in activities that promote creativity and self-expression.

What are some inner child healing techniques?

- Inner child healing techniques may include inner child meditations, guided visualizations, expressive arts therapy, journaling prompts, self-soothing exercises, inner child dialogues, and reparenting practices. These techniques help individuals connect with their inner child, validate their emotions, and provide the nurturing and support needed for healing.

Is inner child work always painful?

- Inner child work can evoke strong emotions and may bring up painful memories or experiences from the past. However, it is also a deeply transformative and healing process that can lead to greater self-awareness, self-compassion, and emotional resilience. With the support of a qualified therapist or supportive community, inner child work can be a powerful tool for growth and healing.

How long does inner child work take?

- The duration of inner child work varies for each individual and depends on factors such as the extent of childhood trauma or wounds, the level of self-awareness and willingness to engage in the process, and the support available. Some individuals may experience significant progress in a relatively short time, while others may require more time and ongoing support to fully heal.

Can I do inner child work on my own?

- While inner child work can be done independently through self-reflection, journaling, and self-guided practices, it is often beneficial to seek the support of a qualified therapist or counselor who specializes in inner child work. A therapist can provide guidance, validation, and a safe space for exploring and processing emotions, facilitating deeper healing and transformation.

What are the long-term benefits of inner child work?

- The long-term benefits of inner child work include increased self-awareness, emotional resilience, and self-compassion, improved relationships and communication skills, greater ability to set boundaries and assert needs, decreased reactivity to triggers or past traumas, and a deeper sense of inner peace, wholeness, and authenticity. Inner child work lays the foundation for lasting personal growth and holistic well-being.

References:

Bradshaw, J. (1992). *Homecoming: Reclaiming and Championing Your Inner Child*. Bantam.

Capacchione, L. (1991). *Recovery of Your Inner Child: The Highly Acclaimed Method for Liberating Your Inner Self*. Simon & Schuster.

Taylor, C. L. (1991). *The Inner Child Workbook: What to Do with Your Past When It Just Won't Go Away*. J.P. Tarcher/Putnam.

Whitfield, C. L. (1991). *Healing the Child Within: Discovery and Recovery for Adult Children of Dysfunctional Families*. Health Communications Inc.

Miller, A. (2008). *The Drama of the Gifted Child: The Search for the True Self*. Basic Books.

Cori, J. L. (2010). *The Emotionally Absent Mother: How to Recognize and Heal the Invisible Effects of Childhood Emotional Neglect*. The Experiment.

Mellody, P. (1989). *Breaking Free: A Recovery Workbook for Facing Codependence*. HarperOne.

Walker, P. (2003). *The Tao of Fully Feeling: Harvesting Forgiveness Out of Blame*. Trafford Publishing.

Tolle, E. (2004). *The Power of Now: A Guide to Spiritual Enlightenment*. New World Library.

Brach, T. (2004). *Radical Acceptance: Embracing Your Life with the Heart of a Buddha*. Bantam.

Further Reading:

Capacchione, L. (2001). *The Creative Journal: The Art of Finding Yourself*. Ohio University Press.

Levine, P. A. (1997). *Waking the Tiger: Healing Trauma*. North Atlantic Books.

Chödrön, P. (2003). *When Things Fall Apart: Heart Advice for Difficult Times*. Shambhala Publications.

Epstein, M. (1995). *Thoughts Without a Thinker: Psychotherapy from a Buddhist Perspective*. Basic Books.

Siegel, D. J. (1999). *The Developing Mind: How Relationships and the Brain Interact to Shape Who We Are*. Guilford Press.

Neff, K. D. (2011). *Self-Compassion: The Proven Power of Being Kind to Yourself*. William Morrow Paperbacks.

Neumann, E. (2011). *The Great Mother: An Analysis of the Archetype*. Princeton University Press.

Johnson, R. A. (1991). *Inner Work: Using Dreams and Active Imagination for Personal Growth*. HarperOne.

Karr-Morse, R., & Wiley, M. S. (2012). *Scared Sick: The Role of Childhood Trauma in Adult Disease*. Basic Books.

Mate, G. (2010). *In the Realm of Hungry Ghosts: Close Encounters with Addiction*. Vintage Canada.

These references and further reading materials offer a comprehensive exploration of inner child work, trauma healing, mindfulness practices, and personal growth. Each resource provides valuable insights and techniques for individuals seeking to embark on their inner healing journey.

www.ingramcontent.com/pod-product-compliance
Lightning Source LLC
LaVergne TN
LVHW021825060526
838201LV00058B/3511